DEADLY SECRETS

U.S. REP. DANA ROHRABACHER on his investigation: "It is astonishing that officials from the Department of Justice and other law enforcement agencies were unwilling to permit congressional investigators to question a former bank robber with a possible connection to a large-scale terrorist attack."

FORMER DEPUTY ASSISTANT FBI DIRECTOR DANNY COULSON: "We have victims here and victims' families, and we don't know the answers. And the answer is frankly a federal grand jury."

U.S. SEN. ORRIN HATCH on the Kenneth Trentadue mystery: "Somebody has not told the truth here and somebody is, in my opinion, covering up."

FEDERAL JUDGE DALE A. KIMBALL on the FBI's conduct: "[W]hile the FBI's failure to discover documents is not necessarily an indication of bad faith, it is puzzling that *so many* documents could be referenced but not produced."

FORENSIC PATHOLOGIST DR. T.K. MARSHALL on the "extra leg" recovered from the Murrah Building: "The working assumption has to be, until excluded, that the leg in question belonged to a bomber."

DEADLY SECRETS

Timothy McVeigh and the
Oklahoma City Bombing

DAVID PAUL HAMMER

AuthorHouse™
1663 Liberty Drive
Bloomington, IN 47403
www.authorhouse.com
Phone: 1-800-839-8640

© 2010 David Paul Hammer. All rights reserved.

No part of this book may be reproduced, stored in a retrieval system, or transmitted by any means without the written permission of the author.

First published by AuthorHouse 4/5/2010

ISBN: 978-1-4520-0364-1 (e)
ISBN: 978-1-4520-0363-4 (sc)
ISBN: 978-1-4520-0362-7 (hc)

Library of Congress Control Number: 2010904034

Printed in the United States of America
Bloomington, Indiana

This book is printed on acid-free paper.

Certain information and passages in this book was previously published and was copyrighted by David Paul Hammer and Jeffery William Paul in 2004.
That material is used here with permission.

Cover photo: 2007 BBC documentary,
Conspiracy Files — Oklahoma City Bombing.

This book is dedicated to
the memory of
Kenneth Michael Trentadue
and to the search for justice.
Someone knows who killed Kenney.

Kenneth Trentadue

The truth is rarely pure and never simple.

— Oscar Wilde

FOREWORD

By Margaret Roberts

This remarkable book speaks for itself. But first, a word about the author is in order. David Paul Hammer is a death row inmate. Credibility is an issue.

Back in the 1980s, I broke a story in Chicago about a death row inmate who claimed he was innocent. Most people who knew what I was working on laughed at me for being so naïve as to think the condemned man's story was worth the enormous amount of time it consumed to investigate. The consensus was: Never believe a prisoner. They're all lying.

Once the story was published, it won prizes in Chicago, and more importantly, influenced the Illinois Supreme Court to reconsider the condemned man's case. Years later, other investigations exonerated him through DNA testing. He was innocent. Other men were proven to be the real murderers. Subsequently, *Newsweek* credited my reporting on that story with changing the death penalty debate in America.

For me, the lesson learned was this: If something is true, even if it comes from death row, it is still the truth. For reasons that you will understand when you read the book, I can't say that I know that David Hammer is telling the truth in this book. Only Hammer knows that. But

I can say this: The astonishing story he says Timothy McVeigh told him is compelling. I can say Hammer's story deserves careful consideration in light of what I regard as the hollow and unconvincing official version of the Oklahoma City Bombing, as told by government prosecutors in the trials of McVeigh and his accomplice Terry Nichols.

I've learned something else about journalism. Trust your gut. I know a lot about this fascinating and still mysterious case. I started digging into it back in 2005 as a producer for the TV crime show *America's Most Wanted*. In the aftermath of the bombing, in 1995, an unidentified suspect known as John Doe No. 2 had become, briefly, the world's most wanted man, an accomplice of McVeigh's, known only from an FBI sketch, who was believed to have somehow escaped the dragnet that caught McVeigh and Nichols.

But something didn't ring right. In short order, the FBI suddenly and improbably canceled its global manhunt, calling John Doe No. 2 a case of eyewitness error. But meanwhile, at least a dozen honest citizens in Oklahoma City and Kansas—people with no apparent reason to lie—continued to insist they had seen the stocky, dark-haired man, who looked nothing like Nichols, with McVeigh. These witnesses were not brought to court to testify for the prosecution. It was as if what they had seen had never happened.

I kept digging. But I never imagined where this story would lead until I heard David Hammer's account of his death row interviews with Timothy McVeigh. According to Hammer, McVeigh disclosed that he was not the mastermind of the bombing, but rather was an undercover government agent in a sting operation that targeted right-wing extremists. But evidently, something went terribly wrong: 168 innocent people wound up dead.

All of this sounds far-fetched. McVeigh certainly had reasons to fabricate a tale of a malevolent government. But upon consideration, his story placed a compelling new light on the John Doe No. 2 mystery. In contrast to the government's account—that McVeigh executed the elaborate delivery of the huge truck bomb single-handedly—McVeigh gave Hammer a much more logistically feasible account, that McVeigh had a support squad of accomplices on the ground in Oklahoma City on April 19, 1995. And he named names.

This book is by no means a mere recounting of prison talk, however. After McVeigh's execution, Hammer, an inmate without ready access to a telephone, the Internet, or face-to-face interviews, undertook a Houdini-like feat: to investigate the validity of McVeigh's story while locked behind bars.

The result is an abundance of evidence, much of it developed through a dogged parallel investigation by another man on the outside, who is central to Hammer's story. He is Jesse C. Trentadue, a lawyer who for many years has pursued the truth about the suspicious death of his brother, a prisoner in federal custody in Oklahoma City the summer after the bombing. Jesse Trentadue and Hammer have come to believe Kenneth Trentadue's death was linked to a government cover-up of federal involvement in the bomb plot.

I won't spoil the book's surprise ending, but suffice it to say, Hammer has far more to lose than gain by writing this story. The Federal Bureau of Prisons prohibits all media interviews with him. With a federal judge's approval, he offered to tell his story about the bombing by videotaped deposition. But the FBI sought and won an order from a higher court to keep Hammer off videotape.

Why would the federal government go to such lengths just to keep an inmate from telling a story? One possible answer is that, against all odds, prison investigative journalist David Paul Hammer is getting close to deeply embarrassing truths regarding the Oklahoma City Bombing.

For now, what is known is that, in the most devastating domestic terrorist strike ever on American soil, investigators didn't seem to investigate every lead, and reporters, for the most part, didn't report anything beyond the government's narrative. And so, strangely, it now falls to David Paul Hammer to break the news from death row.

Here is the news: Contrary to the spin of government insiders who have secrets to hide, the Oklahoma City Bombing case is not closed—not by a long shot. Terrorists who were never brought to justice for the bombing may still be out there. The death of Kenneth Trentadue, who may have been Victim No. 169, remains unsolved. Consider the evidence carefully in the story that follows. Then you be the judge.

PREFACE

I stood at my cell door and watched as prison guards placed restraints on the most infamous Federal Death Row prisoner in history. Timothy James McVeigh exited the deathwatch cell at 3:40 a.m. on Sunday, June 10, 2001. He was dressed in a pair of institutional khaki pants, a white T-shirt, socks and blue slip-on deck shoes. Two correctional officers escorted him. As McVeigh walked down the tier, our eyes met. He nodded once, maintaining his military bearing. I acknowledged him with a similar nod.

No words were spoken, yet McVeigh's meaning was clear to me: "Write the book. Expose the secrets." Timothy McVeigh was only hours from being executed.

This book is based upon my interactions with McVeigh during the 23 months we were housed together on death row at the United States Penitentiary in Terre Haute, Indiana. The book contains firsthand information and accounts provided to me by McVeigh.

When McVeigh was executed, he took many secrets with him. Some of those secrets are contained in this book. In order to obtain them, I was required to barter with McVeigh and take on certain crucial legal issues – notably his desire to give up his appeals and advance his execution date, and his desire not to have his body autopsied. Those legal efforts paved the way for McVeigh's exit from this world on his own terms, within the limits of his situation.

In exchange, McVeigh cooperated with me, knowing full well of my intention to write about him and the Oklahoma City Bombing. I have no doubt that his cooperation was an attempt to control when and where information about him was revealed to the public. Still, our bargain required McVeigh to disclose information that could be verified. And he did that.

Our association was not always amiable. There were intense disputes, allegations of broken promises and even treachery, but in the end the necessity for cooperation won out. Our communications took many forms: debates, arguments, chatter, gossip, explanations, question and answer sessions, and yes, even confessions by McVeigh. Fellow death row inmate Jeffery Paul and others oftentimes witnessed these almost daily exchanges. Paul and I spent more time with McVeigh during the last two years of his life than anyone else. In those months, McVeigh opened up and provided detailed facts that seemed astonishing at the time.

I have honored all aspects of my agreement with McVeigh. He insisted that I delay publishing in book form any of what he revealed until the publication of his biography, *American Terrorist*, in early 2001. That book portrayed McVeigh as the lone-wolf terrorist responsible for planning, financing and carrying out the Oklahoma City Bombing almost single-handedly. That is the story he wanted the public to believe while he was alive.

But to those of us who spent every day with McVeigh, his conflicted emotions were evident in the last months of his life. He was well aware of the growing number of people who didn't buy the government's lone-wolf theory. He was fearful of being labeled a fraud or patsy, of having his image destroyed before his death.

To this day, McVeigh still has many followers and supporters who consider him a hero. I've received death threats from the outside as well as from other inmates because of my writings about McVeigh. I have accepted the risk because I believe that the truth about the Oklahoma City Bombing must be exposed.

I didn't take Timothy McVeigh at his word. With assistance from attorneys and their investigators, and from journalists, I have tried to verify the information McVeigh provided. We have obtained thousands of documents and exhibits via Freedom of Information Act requests and litigation. My attorney or his investigator has interviewed some of the individuals mentioned by McVeigh.

In 1999, at the height of media interest in all things McVeigh, he gave me his Federal Bureau of Prisons ID card to use as proof of my access to him. The ID badge traveled around some in the publishing world, and then was returned to the warden here on Federal Death Row. I kept a digital copy of the image, which is published here for the first time.

One man who is central to my investigation is Jesse C. Trentadue. Jesse and I first met in December 1995, soon after Jesse's brother, Kenneth Michael Trentadue, was killed in his prison cell at the Federal Transfer Center in Oklahoma City. Jesse's investigation of his brother's suspicious death has taken many twists and turns in the past 14 plus years. No one could have scripted the facts he has uncovered, including a link to the bombing case that apparently cost Kenney his life. Jesse's investigation has now established evidence that his brother was murdered by federal agents, engaged in a government cover-up, who mistakenly believed Kenney was an escaped McVeigh accomplice: a man who knew too much.

Jesse's battle with the federal government to uncover the truth behind his brother's death has led him down many paths, but they all lead to Oklahoma City and the bombing. Jesse had no special interest in the bombing case. He never had any reason to think his efforts in his brother's case would land him squarely in the face of a massive cover-up by the federal government. He certainly never would have imagined that Timothy McVeigh himself would reach out from death row with information that would connect the dots in shocking manner between the bombing case and Kenneth Trentadue's death. Yet, as this story will reveal, that is exactly what happened.

I first began writing this manuscript in 2000, with assistance from inmate Jeffery Paul. A version of that writing was published in March 2004 as a book entitled *Secrets Worth Dying For*. Excerpts are included herein.

Following the publication of *Secrets,* some family members of victims who perished in the bombing contacted me. My correspondence with Jannie Coverdale, grandmother of Aaron and Elijah, in particular, has provided me with strength to write this manuscript. I have also been in regular contact with media personalities who have spent years investigating the bombing. They have been invaluable sources of verification and information. My incarceration has slowed the progress of this investigation, but the fruits of our combined efforts are contained in the following pages.

I offer this account of events surrounding the bombing of the Alfred P. Murrah Federal Building in Oklahoma City on April 19, 1995, because the public has just as much right to know Timothy McVeigh's secrets, and the secrets of the U.S. government relating to the bombing, as they have to know the authorized lone-wolf version. I offer this account, as told to me by McVeigh, only for what it is worth. That value is left up to you, the reader, to decide.

— David Paul Hammer
Federal Death Row
Terre Haute, Indiana
April 2010

CHAPTER ONE

OPERATION GOLDEN EAGLE

April 19, 1995: I remember sitting in a solitary cell at the United States Penitentiary in Lompoc, California, listening to my Walkman when news of the Oklahoma City Bombing was broadcast on a local radio station. I didn't have access to any of the television news coverage. The images conjured up in my mind were bad, but nothing in comparison to the actual damage caused by the bombing. The destruction of life and property, the overwhelming sense of loss, were incomprehensible to me. Within two days I had a copy of *The Oklahoman* published on April 20, 1995. A friend in Oklahoma had sent it via overnight mail. I couldn't stop the tears as I read all of the articles, and looked at the photographs of my hometown. One article gave a report as described by a salesman at a car dealership in downtown Oklahoma City. That man was a distant relative of mine. I searched for names of those killed and injured, wondering if anyone I knew or was related to was a victim.

I never dreamed I would one day come to be in a cell next to the man who had committed this atrocity. No one could have ever predicted that a smalltime criminal incarcerated since the age of 19 in the State of Oklahoma, and then transferred into the federal prison system, would eventually be on death row with the Oklahoma City

Bomber. Sometimes the truth really is stranger than fiction. This is one of those times.

Fast-forward four years, to Tuesday morning, July 13, 1999. Timothy McVeigh and I were both inmates at the federal ADX Supermax prison in Florence, Colorado. Often referred to as the "Alcatraz of the Rockies," Supermax is home to the so-called worst of the worst federal prisoners. But until that day, McVeigh and I had virtually no contact.

We were both housed in a secure area of Supermax known as "The Suites" and "Tier 13," a section reserved to isolate inmates even from one another. I was lying on my bunk when the silence was broken by the sounds of electronic clicks and whirs. Locks opened, then sliding doors banged, followed by voices of guards, jangling of keys, and doors being opened.

I heard their steps echo as they walked along the corridor leading to my cell. Two officers approached the outer door. Another guard monitored them via a video camera and closed circuit TV screen. Some unknown signal was given, buttons were pushed, and the control room officer far away opened my outer cell door electronically.

I sat up on the side of my bunk. Two guards stepped into the isolated area in front of the cell. They were senior officers, one being a lieutenant. Another officer stood watch, armed with a 36-inch riot baton sporting a round silver ball on its tip (known to all inmates as the "rib-splitter").

The lieutenant said: "Hammer, you need to put on your jumpsuit and shoes. We were told to bring you to the hospital for an examination." Having been given a direct order, I obeyed. While rapidly changing from my sweat pants into the requisite orange jumpsuit and tennis shoes, I questioned the officers about the unexpected trip to the hospital. In prison it is all about routine. Medical visits are by appointment unless it is an emergency. Their response: "We are just following orders."

I dressed. They ordered me to back up against the cell bars. They handcuffed my hands behind my back and placed leg shackles on my ankles. The lieutenant held my hands immobile. A signal was given. The cell door slid open. I was instructed to walk backwards. Doors opened and closed. I was leaving that cell for the last time.

I remained silent, as required, during the walk. To my surprise, we entered a door leading not to the hospital, but rather to the institution's receiving and discharge area. Something unusual was happening. Various members of the prison's administration were present, along with an alarming number of security staff dressed in camouflage garb. Excitement, tension and a sense of the unexpected were in the air.

After I was placed into an open-faced enclosure with steel bars, my restraints were removed and I was ordered to strip. That procedure required that I first face forward with my arms and hands extended in front, palms down and fingers spread open. Naked as the day I came into this world, I stood as my hands, armpits, mouth, nose and ears were checked. I was then required to bend forward and run my fingers through my hair. After standing upright I was ordered to lift up my penis, and then my testicles. I was then instructed to turn around and face the back wall, to lift up each foot and wiggle my toes. Last, but not least, I was required to bend over, reach back with both hands, and spread my buttocks. Then, while in that position, I was told to cough twice.

Next, I was escorted to another holding cell, where I was allowed to dress in a pair of pull-on khaki pants and top that resembled pajamas, socks and deck shoes. I was placed in full transport restraints. Those consisted of leg irons on my ankles and a waist chain applied like a belt. Handcuffs were inserted through the waist chain and then onto my wrists. A device known as a black box was fitted over the handcuffs, covering the keyholes. The waist chain buckle was inserted through the black box, and a large padlock was applied to secure the restraints in place. These restraints hold your hands immobile in front at waist level. This is a most painful position to be in for more than a few minutes.

I was then placed into yet another holding cell, where I heard Timothy McVeigh call my name from the next cell. "Hammer, I hear you're from Oklahoma," McVeigh said. I replied that I was. He then stated: "I hope there's no hard feelings." Our exchange was interrupted when an officer ordered us to remain silent. There was a loud disturbance as another prisoner, Anthony Battle, was brought into a holding cell. He was already in full restraints, but complaining bitterly about how tightly they had been applied. Battle received a death sentence for killing a guard at the federal prison in Atlanta. Our destination was now clear: We three all had federally imposed death sentences, and rumors had been ongoing for months about the Bureau of Prison's new Federal Death Row unit being activated.

We were escorted from Supermax one at a time by a four-man team, while under the watchful lens of a video camera, through an underground garage and onto a prison transport bus. Officers armed with riot batons, gas masks and hand-held canisters of tear gas were stationed in the aisle of the bus just opposite of where each of us was seated. One officer for each inmate, with his baton ready to strike at any sign of trouble.

Prison transport buses are designed as rolling fortresses. An officer with a shotgun was stationed in the rear of the bus in a secure area. Through a turret-type structure, he was capable of firing his weapon anywhere into the prisoners' section.

The front of the bus, where the driver and a lieutenant were positioned, was separated from the prisoners' section by grates and a steel door. These officers were armed with side arms and other weapons, including an M-16 type of weapon. A third officer stood on the steps of the bus with his back to the closed door. We proceeded in a caravan of vehicles that included two in the lead and two following.

In addition, Colorado state troopers and a military-style vehicle with a machine gun on top escorted the bus. All officers wore bulletproof vests and helmets. The transport was under the direct supervision of the captain of security from the ADX and others from Washington, D.C.

As the bus traveled to the airport in Pueblo, Colorado, McVeigh and I talked about the beauty of the land – and about our suspected destination. The guards stood at stoical attention, batons raised in anticipation of trouble.

Two guards standing beside McVeigh and me began a conversation. One announced: "Y'all three should be executed on pay-per-view TV. Hammer, you and Battle as the warm-up to the main event. McVeigh, you will be the main attraction and you should go last." The second guard replied: "Yeah, and all the proceeds from the telecast should go to law enforcement."

McVeigh responded: "That sounds like a plan. And what's an execution without beer and popcorn? Who gets the profit from the concession stands?"

"It won't be you, McVeigh," his guard responded. Little did either of them know at the time that during the weeks leading up to McVeigh's execution, an entertainment company would litigate in federal court for the right to broadcast his execution on the Internet. And that hundreds of victims' family members would watch McVeigh's execution via a closed-circuit feed into a location in Oklahoma City. No live at five Internet coverage, but a spectacle all the same.

At the airport in Pueblo, "Con-Air," the U.S. Marshals Service federal transport plane, was waiting with a flight crew and a cadre of deputies. Four other condemned men from Texas were already on the plane when we boarded. Within minutes we were airborne. I sat in the middle seat of a row over the wing. McVeigh sat across the aisle. Despite an order not to talk, we had lengthy conversation during the flight.

I am a native Oklahoman, born and raised there. I attended school in Oklahoma City, where my family lived for many years. Being in such close proximity to Timothy McVeigh, arguably the most hated man in the country, presented a unique situation. What were my feelings supposed to be about this person? Where did my loyalties lie?

The U.S. Marshals transport center and planes, as well as the Bureau of Prison's Federal Transfer Center, are based in Oklahoma City. Several of the deputies on this flight knew me from their previous employment with the Oklahoma City Police Department or the Oklahoma Department of Corrections. During the flight, two of these deputies began to taunt McVeigh with stories of my past misdeeds and with exaggerated tales of violence attributed to me. They informed him that I'd been sentenced to death for killing a federal prisoner. They made sure he got the impression that because I was an Oklahoman with a history of extreme violence, he had better watch out. I attempted to reassure him that he had nothing to fear from me.

Our plane next made a stop in Little Rock, Arkansas, where more prisoners joined the flight. Deputies now reassigned seats in a staggered seating arrangement. McVeigh was near the front of the plane. Jeff Paul, who had boarded in Arkansas, was in the middle. I was towards the rear. Conducting any conversation was difficult, but, filled with nervous energy, some tried. Most of the men were anxious about flying in such an aged aircraft.

At one point during the flight, the deputies passed out granola bars and bottles of water. I passed on the snacks, but, with assistance, I did down a couple of bottles of water. Watching the others attempt to eat their snacks was amusing. Because of the restraints, guys would have to bend over at the waist all the way down in their seats. Their heads popped up and down like gophers in their holes.

After about an hour of flying the plane began its descent. Even with my limited view it was clear we were landing in Indiana. The airport was one used primarily by airfreight carriers, not commercial passenger service. It was bordered by farms, corn crops and grain silos.

Arriving in Indiana was like nothing most of the prisoners had seen before. None were greenhorns when it came to heavy security precautions. That's a given when one has received a death sentence. But this scene was something straight out of a Hollywood movie. Once on the ground, the plane was surrounded by an array of law enforcement vehicles and no fewer than 50 officers armed with automatic rifles and side arms, and dressed in full body armor. They wore black fatigues with utility belts, gas canisters and an assortment of equipment affixed to their belts. The officers took up various positions securing a perimeter with each facing away from the plane on alert for any type of a threat.

A second contingent of heavily armed officers, with their weapons pointing directly at the rear exit door of the plane, took up their positions to await our departure. A portable rolling staircase was pushed up to the doorway. Transport buses were pulled into place. The first three inmates to exit were Battle, McVeigh and I. A deputy escorted each of us to the rear of the plane while holding onto the waist chain. A second deputy compared our names, numbers and faces to a master list with photographs. Then we were required to give our date of birth. One can only assume these measures were in place to ensure that no imposter sneaked his way onto Federal Death Row.

At the bottom of the staircase there was a gap of about eight inches from the last step to the ground. That wouldn't have been such a big deal, but each inmate had leg restraints on his ankles. Not to worry, because at the bottom of the stairs awaited a welcome party of four BOP officers dressed in black ninja-type garb and armed with batons. The first guard would grab a fistful of shirt at the collar and give a quick jerk forward, right off the steps. A knee well placed in the groin from the same guard did help to steady us while another guard to the side ground his fingers into our upper arms. One guard on each side made certain we didn't lose our balance. Then we were pat searched yet again. With officers holding us by the waist chain in back, and one on each side, still applying pressure to our arms, and a fourth officer with baton raised, we walked the distance of about 25 feet to the bus.

I passed a group of administrative types in suits. Several people were standing around taking photographs and videotaping each of us. All staff, officers and suits had head and chin radios allowing instant communication with those in command. We learned later that the Justice Department and BOP had dubbed this massive transfer of 20 federal inmates from all across the country Operation Golden Eagle.

Once the buses were loaded, they crept slowly onto the highway, where, to our surprise, more manpower joined in. An additional three dozen local police patrol cars, Indiana state troopers, and Vigo County Sheriff's Department cruisers with lights and sirens on, accompanied by another dozen or so unmarked sedans with bubble lights on their dashes, all fell in with the convoy. A helicopter flew overhead directing drivers to clear the roads. Vans loaded with SWAT members paced the buses at a suitable distance.

Our journey from the airport to the U.S. Penitentiary, Terre Haute, took approximately 20 minutes. The cruisers darted up ahead and then pulled back, weaving through the procession chaotically as it sped through town. Through back roads bordered by cornfields, onto city streets, onto Interstate 70 for a short distance, back onto more city streets, we traveled. Onlookers, forced to the side of streets, craned their necks to see the spectacle, a parade of the unusual. They pointed and stared. Some had exited their cars and were sitting on hoods of their vehicles waiting for the roads to clear. Most of the traffic had been eliminated as city police blocked intersections with emergency lights warning all of our presence.

McVeigh summed it up this way: 'I was surprised to realize we would be driving right through Terre Haute. We actually blew past a Wal-Mart and a Burger King. I couldn't believe it. I had assumed it would be a rural route. That would be logical from a threat-management point of view. Two well-armed SWAT vans with close air support could easily deal with trouble in a restrictive environment and protect the public effectively. When compared with the resources they must have spent, as well as the inconvenience to the public, it's obvious the operation was a prison orchestrated show, to assure and dazzle the country."

Did I mention the media? The caravan was followed by a train of media that had more than a little difficulty staying close enough to videotape much. The buses' tinted windows kept the public and reporters from seeing inside. As we arrived at the prison another group of media and TV news crews was waiting on private property across the road. They had long-range video cameras mounted on tripods and various recording equipment. One reporter appeared disheveled and very animated as he stood talking to those gathered by a news van and pointing at us. Possibly, he was trying to spot the infamous passenger, Timothy McVeigh, who at the time was staring back through the tinted glass with an amused smile on his face.

McVeigh seemed genuinely pleased by the interest. Prison officials had alerted the media to the arrival of the Terre Haute Twenty, as we were quickly labeled by various reports.

At 3:30 p.m. the buses stopped at the back gate of the prison. Out stepped a group of 21 BOP officers dressed in full riot gear and black military fatigues, which seemed to be the order of the day. These men, all the size of professional football players, were members of the prison's Special Operations and Response Team, known as the SORT Team, or, by prisoners, as the Goon Squad. They wore helmets with face guards attached, and dark sunglasses, and most held long batons. They filed onto the buses, stomping their combat boots in perfect synch.

Processing had begun. In order to get the full effect of the SORT team lieutenant's orders, close your eyes and imagine a military drill instructor with a puffed out chest, red cheeks and a vacant look in his eyes as he screams these words: "You are in the custody of the Federal Bureau of Prisons. You do not look up. You do not move unless told to do so, and you'd better keep your shit-eating mouths shut!"

The lieutenant then turned and asked the gun-cage officer who the "problem children" were. The guard pointed to Battle and explained that he had been complaining about the tightness of his restraints, and at me, stating that I had a medical condition, referring to my diabetes. Battle was removed from the bus first and received some special abuse by the Goon Squad. Obviously his reputation as a guard killer preceded his arrival. I heard one guard say: "I'll show you how a dog lives and dies." It had been widely reported that during his trial, Battle stated that the officer he killed had lived like a dog and died like one.

As we exited the bus, another search was conducted. McVeigh recalled: "During the pat down, I felt a tingle from the hair on the back of my head standing on end. It was a familiar feeling, and when I turned around to move on, I glanced up and spotted a sniper in the tower leaning out, following the activity with his rifle."

Some of the black inmates commented about Indiana having once been a stronghold for the Ku Klux Klan. They wondered aloud if McVeigh would get the red carpet treatment, or at least a cup of coffee and a sympathetic nod from the "good 'ole boys."

That didn't seem likely. Almost from the beginning of the operation, the officers had been playing upon McVeigh's fears of being sexually assaulted – and they were using my name. They played mind games with McVeigh by talking loudly about my past, and me being from Oklahoma. As I watched McVeigh being processed, I could see he was rattled. The sheer rage on the faces of the staff members and guards was remarkable. Several came to leer at McVeigh for no reason other than a first glimpse of the Oklahoma City Bomber. While McVeigh was undergoing a strip search under the watchful eyes of staff and fellow inmates, his head was held against the concrete so hard as to warrant intervention by a supervisor, who told guards: "You better calm down or you'll be a part of breaking news." Trying to make light of the situation, McVeigh commented: "Looks like the Klan turned into ZOG." The right-wing phraseology was short for Zionist occupied government.

Each of us was photographed, finger printed, strip-searched, and had our scars and tattoos documented. Forms were signed. Restraints were reapplied. We were led into a holding area, and then into cells.

Having been in prison for over 30 years, I've seen just about everything you can imagine in these places. I know the kind of mind games used by the guards: shake, rattle and roll. They shake you physically, rattle your brain, and roll your ass off to the cellblock. But this operation was something else. I was thankful the guy with the video camera was right on scene to capture events on tape.

In the holding cell, in groups of five or six, we had our first opportunity to talk out of the presence of guards. I told McVeigh he shouldn't pay any attention to what the guards said about me. That we are all in the same boat, since the government was intent on executing each of us. Jeff Paul and several other inmates were also present. Introductions were made. McVeigh had never previously been held in a cell with other inmates. He was nervous, but bantered with us. At one point he half-joked that there wouldn't be any conjugal visits during recreation.

One at a time we were then taken to an office about the size of a closet. Two beefy guards escorted us and then stood watch over the encounter as a staffer sat behind a desk writing. Jeff Paul recalled his experience this way: "They set me down and this one guard sort of worked his way behind the chair. His gut was literally pushing flat against the back of my head. The other guard stood, blocking the door with his rib-splitter baton ready to do its damage. The desk jockey tells me that I need to sign for a copy of the prison rules and regulations after asking me a ton of questions they already knew the answers to. The hack at the door says: 'Now I'm gonna hand you a pen. You can stand up and put your 'X' on the form, but if you do anything funny with that pen, I'm going to crack your fucking head right down the middle.'

"At this point, my nerves are about shot and I don't know what he means by funny, so when he puts the pen down, I just sit there, looking at it. After a long wait, he asks what the hell my problem is, and I say, 'Well, I'm sore already. I feel like this is a lose-lose situation, and, I figure if you're going to bust me up, I'd rather get it for nothing, than something, so my Mom can sue your ass, cause I don't know your definition of funny and I ain't touching that pen.'

"The guy blinks, then actually laughs and steps back, saying, 'Just sign it, all right?' So, I did, carefully, and was then informed that they had run out of copies of the rules manual and I'd have to get it later. Typical."

Meanwhile, back in the holding cell, numerous conversations ensued, with the main topic being executions and the death penalty. Views ran the spectrum from "God will save me" to "I'm innocent, but have faith in the system and hope that each of the cocksuckers involved dies a slow and painful death before going straight to hell. The sooner the better."

McVeigh remained silent on this issue, but when I prompted him he commented: "All I have to say is that the official score is 168 to 1.

I'm up." After an uncomfortable pause, I told him: "Huh, well, I guess they can't kill you more than once."

Paul and McVeigh ended up discussing the weapons carried by the officers throughout the day. Paul, having grown up in the South and being familiar with guns and the gun show circuit that McVeigh seemed to like so much, was able to participate in these conversations. Most of the guys present were impressed with McVeigh's uncanny recap of weapons specifications down to the minutest detail. I joked with McVeigh that he must have been popping a bottle of aspirin a day while he memorized *Soldier of Fortune* magazine.

By the late afternoon we were all tired and hungry. None of us had eaten a meal since early that morning. McVeigh leaned across Paul towards the door of the holding cell and yelled: "Take us to our fucking cells."

The response was rapid. Several guards opened the door cursing. They grabbed Jeff Paul by the front of his shirt, jerking him down the hallway. He recalled what happened next: "It was real quick. I didn't even get a chance to say anything before I was spinning. They rushed me right into the doorframe of the hallway and bounced me off of the wall, over and over, dragging me back the way we'd come in. Out of the corner of my eye, I saw the guy with the video camera, but he was pointing it straight down at the floor. I yelled at him: 'What, you don't want to get this on film?' "If he said anything back, I was gone before he opened his mouth, so I wouldn't know."

Back in the holding cell, we voiced our protest over what had just happened. We told the staff that Paul hadn't done anything. When a guard asked sarcastically, "Then who did?" there was only silence. No one was going to point the finger at McVeigh.

Jeff Paul was the youngest man in the group being transported that day. I think that's part of the reason he had been singled out all day long. The guards were wound up real tight. They manhandled Paul back outside the building and onto the bus, where he sat through a verbal assault, punctuated by fingers poking his forehead and the rib-splitting baton grinding into his side. Shortly, the lieutenant arrived and calmed the situation. Paul was asked who caused the trouble in the cell, but he said nothing.

Back in the holding cell, I watched McVeigh, who had been quiet as a church mouse since causing the guards to snatch up Paul. It didn't escape notice that this so-called badass bomber was as passive as a virgin on her wedding night. He let an innocent kid take the rap for his attempt to impress the fellas. Not a good start.

In short order, we were each loaded back onto the bus, nodding at Paul with a silent show of support as we passed him in his seat.

The group of guards fell back into formation around the bus as it traveled about a hundred yards to another building. Welcome to Federal Death Row, better known to its residents as Dog Unit. We were offloaded two at a time, issued red jumpsuits, restrained, and placed into our cells, where the heat index stood at 115 degrees that afternoon.

Our first meal was hot pork and potatoes. Everyone was exhausted, but it was way too hot to sleep. On our small black-and-white TVs, we watched the day's events unfold on the local news. The star attraction was McVeigh. USP-Terre Haute was his new home. Operation Golden Eagle was a success.

CHAPTER TWO

Dog Unit

Despite the exhaustion of that first day in transit, none of us could sleep. McVeigh, like the rest of us, found himself nursing wrists that were bruised and swollen from the long hours in handcuffs and the black box. From cell to cell advice and remedies were passed along. We quickly found that communication was easy if we talked out of the back windows of our cells. The cooler air that came with darkness brought a much needed respite from the heat.

In short order we began to get our bearings and discovered who was housed in the cells around us. I listened to tales of the day's events as described by one and then another of the men around me. As it turned out there had been two planes with passengers headed for Dog Unit. The U.S. Marshals Service had driven three men to Terre Haute in a van. The second plane had flown in from the East, retrieving inmates along the way.

McVeigh, Paul and I were housed in a row of cells on the top tier. McVeigh and I were eager to hear from Paul about what had transpired after he was snatched up from the holding cell. Jeff joked about it, and that helped alleviate some of the tension. McVeigh told him: "You took a good one for the team." That was the beginning of the association between McVeigh, Paul and me.

That first night also brought the late local news on TV. In an on-the-street interview, a local man, whose property was next to the prison, was asked about his new infamous neighbor, Timothy McVeigh. The man said something to the effect of: "A good ole' fashion hangin'" was in order.

The row erupted in a roar of laughter and a bit of outrage. Some of the black inmates began yelling for McVeigh, telling him that he had been kicked out of the conspiracy, referring jokingly to the "white conspiracy." McVeigh responded: "If that cornhusker can figure out how to tie a noose, I'll put my neck into it."

The next day, with temperatures on the rise, no one slept in. It quickly became apparent that the previous occupants had vacated our cells in haste. The floors were sticky and dirty, and the grime was corner to corner. The cell walls had cracked off-white paint and were spotted with dark stains of unknown origin. There were splotches and smears of food sticking to the wall. The stench was overpowering in some cells. The porcelain fixtures, consisting of a sink and toilet, were encrusted with layer after layer of rust and bright orange-colored streaks. In one of his less guarded moments, McVeigh dropped his soldier routine and described the place as a "fuckin' dump."

Many cells were being overrun with ants. The source of these insects was quickly determined to be what at first glance seemed to be roach traps. Upon closer inspection, these little cardboard cartons contained pieces of candy or rotting food. The heat had putrefied the contents. Some very offensive remarks were directed towards the Cuban inmates who had left these contraptions behind, for even in prison, manners go a long way. We later learned from reading a book by Professor Mark Hamm, entitled *The Abandoned Ones,* that these cartons were impromptu altars used by the Cuban inmates, some of whom practiced the Santeria religion. They possibly left the altars behind to benefit those condemned to death. Gestures of goodwill, perhaps, and not the acts of disrespect as were first perceived.

But the most pressing problem was the heat. With no air circulation, the heat seemed to settle in the lungs, sapping the body of all strength. McVeigh, weakened by the steady stream of sweat pouring out of him, had a very difficult time drinking the water. It was occasionally the brownish color of tea and had the aroma of spoilt eggs. He vomited repeatedly, loud enough to get Jeff Paul's attention. When urged to seek medical attention for the dehydration and vomiting, McVeigh refused. I gave him some cherry-flavored cough drops to kill the taste of the water.

Confined to our cells, most inmates were dressed in nothing but underwear. The guards walked around out of uniform in T-shirts and with towels soaked in cold water around their necks. Two days into our stay on Dog Unit, an inmate in the prison's general population died of heat stroke.

After about a week, recreation time was approved. That morning, we were all up, excited to be leaving our cells for exercise and a shower. To our surprise, that would have to wait. One at a time, we were escorted to the back of the unit and into an indoor exercise area, but not for recreation. Once there, we were ordered to strip out of the soiled and dirty clothing that we had worn for several days without the benefit of a shower. We were ordered to place the dirty clothing into an extra large zip-top bag that an officer was holding. The bag also contained a blue index card with each inmate's name, number and photograph. We each then had to take a new washcloth and rub it on our armpits and genitals. The washcloth was added to the plastic bag and sealed. Our scent had been preserved. The bags were to be stored in some freezer in the bowels of the prison in case one of us ever escaped. We were told this would serve as a scent reference for the hounds. McVeigh jokingly wondered how much his dirty undershorts would sell for once he had been executed. In all of my many years in prison I've never seen anything quite like it. Not once afterwards did any other prisoner arriving on the row have to contribute to the scent pool.

The first day of outside recreation was loud and boisterous. This was our first opportunity to stand face-to-face and converse in a normal voice with one another. We recreated in groups of five or six, yet separated in individual cages. The heat was hovering close to 100 degrees, so most everyone stripped down to T-shirts and boxers, if they had been allowed to purchase them from the commissary by then.

Jeff Paul and McVeigh spent their time doing pushups and talking. Both were into staying slim and trim at all cost. Soon there were bursts of laughter from several men. Prisoners who had leaned their backs against the cages had criss-cross rusty metal stains emblazoned across the backs of their shirts, or skin if they had removed shirts. They looked as if they had been afflicted with some unknown disease

Early into our stay on the row, our clothing turned pink. That included our bed sheets, underwear, T-shirts and socks. The death row jumpsuits we were required to wear had been dyed red by the manufacturing process. The garments were all of awkward sizes and bled red dye when worn in the hot sun and heat. Sweating caused the dye to turn our clothing what McVeigh termed "fairy pink." It was a ridiculously funny sight, 20 of the so-called most dangerous men in America, including the notorious Timothy McVeigh, standing in the rec yard in pink boxer shorts. The pink color was even worse after our clothing was laundered for the first time. All clothing was washed together with the red jumpsuits, so pink remained the color of death row for many months afterwards.

Our conversations in the recreation cages centered on a few themes. McVeigh loved to speak on warfare, weapons and explosives. He had newsletters and magazines such as *Resistance* sent into death row. One book that he insisted Paul read was entitled *Unintended Consequences*. McVeigh stated that if he'd read this novel before the *Turner Diaries*, things might have turned out differently. The book described a grass-roots movement that used strategic assassinations to overthrow the federal government. McVeigh signed a copy of it for Paul.

McVeigh and Paul liked to watch the same movies or TV shows, or read the same books, and then discuss them in the rec yard. McVeigh preferred political thrillers. He also liked to impress Paul by weaving elaborate escape scenarios. "I could pop this whole unit open with a well armed five-man team," McVeigh claimed.

We got glimpses of his peculiarities too. His public image meant everything to McVeigh. Anything that made him appear weak or incompetent had to be avoided at all cost. He became infuriated when the media reported on spelling errors in letters he wrote. He would not keep a dictionary in his cell. Instead, he would borrow one from Paul or me and then return it as quickly as possible. He had pornography sent to the prison, but he had Jeff Paul keep it in his cell. When McVeigh got sick, instead of seeing the doctor, he usually would ask other inmates to sign up for sick call, represent his symptoms, and obtain medication for him, leaving no paper trail.

Beyond our small circle of three, McVeigh, in his quirky way, made an effort to reach out to the other men living on the row too. When television broadcasts featured him, he would routinely receive piles of mail, most of it from women. Many of the letters contained sexually explicit scenarios, and most were doused with perfume. One woman from Germany wrote McVeigh short-story-length letters monthly, detailing her fantasies.

McVeigh would take these letters to recreation and pass them out to the guys. He would read aloud some of the more twisted letters to fellow prisoners in their cages. Guards standing watch would pull up a chair and listen to McVeigh's groupies' letters being read and discussed. The letters would be divided up and some taken back to the cells for use as air fresheners or private fantasy material.

McVeigh has oftentimes been characterized as charismatic. In fact, he was a very socially awkward man in a place filled with social misfits. In conversations, he would figuratively drown outside his comfort zone of political rhetoric, military or militia oriented topics. He took a lot of ribbing, especially when it came to the subject of women.

McVeigh would listen raptly to the guys telling stories about girlfriends and exploits with women. McVeigh's naïveté' was obvious from the questions he asked. The men would openly call him "virgin McVeigh" until he would be red-faced with embarrassment. Sometimes they confronted him with a question that haunted McVeigh and turned his forehead into a flaming red crinkle. How could McVeigh, whose face, name and story had been plastered all over the world for years during his trial and incarceration, explain why not one single woman had come forward to acknowledge a romantic or sexual relationship with him?

He'd try to stay cool and joke his way out of this by saying: "You should read the *National Enquirer*." Under serious questioning by Paul and me, he admitted both to being a virgin and to not having much experience with women.

When we encouraged him to correspond with some of the women who had written to him, McVeigh replied that he wouldn't waste his time. Any woman who wasn't a virgin until marriage was a slut, in

McVeigh's view. Professional women were stupid. So were independent women, and they never knew their place. Any woman who appeared overtly sexual was dirty.

There are few secrets in prison. When some of McVeigh's private habits became known, they fueled even more speculation about his sexuality. McVeigh would completely shave off all of his body hair, including under his arms, pubic hair and the hair on his legs and torso. This was difficult to do in prison because razors are only issued while showering, and your shower time is strictly limited. Additionally, you are limited to using one or two disposable razors of poor quality. Shaving one's face with these is torture. But the guards made it known that McVeigh shaved his whole body. When Paul and I asked about this, he said it was a practice he had picked up during the Gulf War because of the sand fleas. When we explained to him that such a habit in prison might be viewed as something else, he just shrugged it off.

McVeigh had another odd habit. He would regularly make offers to purchase used boxer shorts from some of the guys on the row. He would pay twice as much as what new boxers from the commissary were sold for. However, he had one very specific requirement. He only wanted boxers that had been worn and not laundered. At least two of the men on Dog Unit routinely sold McVeigh their dirty boxers. It didn't take long for McVeigh's strange request to become common knowledge. When I quizzed him about this he admitted to having a penchant for body odors. He wouldn't get any more specific than that. However, he insisted he was not gay and that one inclination had nothing to do with the other.

A wiser man in McVeigh's high-profile position would have had the good sense to keep his head down and keep quiet. Not Tim. He wasn't dumb, but his mouth was his worst enemy.

One problem was that McVeigh was new to incarceration. He was just plain ignorant of the realities of prison life. Jeff Paul and I tried to bring him up to speed, but he wasn't a quick study. He called a fellow Hispanic inmate a "wetback" to his face, and set off a firestorm of controversy. He called fellow inmates "punks" without even realizing that in prison this term means a submissive homosexual, or that calling someone a punk is a killing offense. He referred to the African-American community in Buffalo as "porch monkeys," which almost caused a race riot on the row, where most inmates were black. Yet McVeigh seemed oblivious to the fact that any one of these insults could easily have resulted in a foot-long shank sticking into his chest.

Trouble was coming. The only question was when.

Beneath the surface of his cool, Timothy McVeigh was dwelling on the thought that someone was going to "get" him. He would whisper his fears to Paul in private. "All it would take is a drop of my blood on their hands to get on the cover of *Time*, and they know it," McVeigh said.

He was particularly fearful of me, though I meant him no harm. During this time, he obtained a copy of a federal court opinion that made him even more paranoid about me. The opinion by U.S. District Court Judge Frank H. Seay described me as a "clever, manipulative, dangerous, violent criminal" and cited my transgressions inside prison, including "using a weapon to take an Oklahoma State Penitentiary prison psychologist hostage."

Jeff Paul attempted to reassure his friend that he had nothing to fear from me. But McVeigh insisted that he wasn't going to "let anyone rock him to sleep." He set out to arrange a cell move.

Paul warned McVeigh that if he requested to move it would open him up to what he feared most: others perceiving him as weak. So, McVeigh placed a telephone call to his lawyers and had them contact prison officials, who then facilitated McVeigh's movement to the opposite end of the tier from my cell. Then, McVeigh and Paul realized they would no longer be in the same recreation rotation, so McVeigh requested that Paul be moved into the empty cell next to him. The request was approved. McVeigh and Paul were now housed in cells 39 and 40. But unfortunately for McVeigh, he had just orchestrated disaster.

McVeigh's deep-seated fear of being raped in prison was a major factor contributing to his paranoia. He would often ask questions about prison sex. Jeff Paul advised him on how to avoid predators intent on manipulation or game playing for sex. I told him how to fight back if confronted in a group situation, and how to avoid placing himself at risk for being sexually abused. Since I knew he feared me in particular, I straight out informed McVeigh I had no intentions of assaulting him in any way, and that I most definitely wasn't into forced sex. But words didn't help. McVeigh was a prisoner of his fear.

Each time the prison would go on lock-down, rumors detailing the reasons why, including assaults, rapes or killings, would run rampant. McVeigh would become very quiet and nervous with each re-telling from the guards of how some incident went down. He was, no doubt, thinking it could easily be him getting carried out on a gurney with his throat cut. He said he wasn't afraid of dying, but that it wouldn't do for America's future if he, who was part of history, were taken down by a crackhead trying to take his ass, literally. To his way of thinking, the possibility of losing face was terrifying.

Showering was a particular concern of McVeigh's. In order to ensure that we were all allowed to shower on our assigned day, the guards working the unit took it upon themselves to shower us two at a time. Once in the showers, each prisoner was locked inside his respective stall alone. But McVeigh felt threatened and wanted to shower by himself. He asked his lawyers to address the issue on his behalf. Unfortunately for him, the guards and inmates all learned of his actions. Not only was he seen as weak, but some of the guards vowed revenge.

Then it happened. In September 1999, trouble came when Timothy McVeigh least expected it.

With his move to cell 39, McVeigh had positioned himself at the end of a tier, next to the stairs and across from the walkway leading onto the side of the unit housing a group of Cuban detainees being held by the Immigration and Naturalization Service. Several times each day, guards making their rounds would rattle our cell doors to make certain they were shut and locked. Each door was opened and closed manually using a key. The tiers were not monitored by any video cameras or alarms.

During one of his rounds, a guard who despised McVeigh unlocked his door while rattling it. McVeigh had no way of knowing his cell was unlocked. The guard unlocked the door of two Cuban inmates, and instructed them to have their way with McVeigh, but not to harm him physically. Both the Cubans were known for having assaulted and raped other inmates. They were now being allowed to do so with the blessing of the guard.

The Cuban inmates entered McVeigh's cell and sexually assaulted him. He didn't fight back or raise much of a commotion. The attack was overheard by some, including Jeff Paul and me. We held mirrors out our cell doors, and we could see the front of McVeigh's cell. In broken English, we heard one of the assailants demand that McVeigh perform oral sex on them. They also threatened him: "We come back and kill you if you tell!" They slapped and punched him before leaving the cell and closing the door.

McVeigh wouldn't answer us when we asked if he was all right. He didn't leave his cell for several days. We finally got him to come out where we could talk in private. After we confronted him with what we had seen and heard, McVeigh told us what had happened. He attempted to put on a brave face, but he was rocked to his very soul. His biggest fear had become a reality. He asked Paul to make him a shank so that if they ever came back he would be able to defend himself. He swore us to secrecy, but knew that others on the tier had seen and heard what happened to him.

I figured that McVeigh would alert the authorities to what had happened. But he didn't want anyone to know: no reports, no lawyers' involvements. His manhood had been assaulted, his pride injured. But that was nothing in comparison to the humiliation he would endure if the media discovered what had happened. His pride just couldn't stand that. Such an attack on his reputation would have been worse than the physical and sexual attacks. He told us just that.

The stage was set for a death row bargain between McVeigh and me.

Timothy McVeigh needed protection, and he knew it. He needed protection from guards, other inmates, the excesses of his own ego, and certainly from the public revelation of what had just happened to him.

For my part, I needed the truth from Timothy McVeigh for a book I wanted to write about the Oklahoma City bombing: a book that would go beyond the unconvincing lone-wolf scenario McVeigh and the U.S. government were so carefully constructing.

Jeff Paul and I showed McVeigh a letter from the *National Enquirer* tabloid newspaper, wherein the sum of $10,000 was mentioned for information on the infamous Oklahoma City Bomber. I told him: "I think the public might be interested in knowing that you have been turned into a prison sex slave and how the guards turn a blind eye to your plight."

We agreed to cooperate. A most unusual literary collaboration was formed.

As McVeigh told Jeff Paul: "A deal with the devil you know beats the unknown and uncontrolled."

3

CHAPTER THREE

AGENT McVEIGH

At the outset I must state in unequivocal terms that I have no personal knowledge about events surrounding the Oklahoma City Bombing. The account that follows is based exclusively upon information provided by Timothy McVeigh, and document reviews and investigations conducted to verify McVeigh's secrets.

I cannot attest to the veracity of McVeigh's claims. Many were the times he and I argued, when I challenged his version of events, or he contradicted himself or changed his story, as he often did. McVeigh could be an enigma. His motives were never obvious. Knowing he was a master at spinning his views complicated my efforts to compile the story and, later, to investigate it.

This I do know: In contrast to the image he cultivated, and federal prosecutors made almost indelible, Timothy McVeigh was no mastermind. Tim had some fine qualities. He was able to follow instructions to the tee. But his intelligence was average at best. His communication skills were limited, and he definitely was not a leader.

As for the story McVeigh told, what I can state with certainty is that much of the information provided by McVeigh contained here has now been confirmed. In the earlier version of this book, I intentionally left out many facts because I had no independent verification of them. Now I do.

The most sensational aspect of McVeigh's story is that he named names of specific people he said were his accomplices in the bombing. I have reported the names of these people, and their alleged actions, just as McVeigh told the story to me. It must be remembered, however, that none of these people has ever been charged in connection with the bombing. All of them must be presumed innocent under the law unless proven otherwise. From my prison cell, I had no opportunity to interview any of them.

I am not here to accuse anyone, only to report what McVeigh said, and critically examine the story through documents and information available to me. This is Timothy McVeigh's account of the Oklahoma City Bombing as he told it to me.

The story opens in 1991, at Camp McCall, the Army's headquarters for Special Forces training on the grounds of Fort Bragg, North Carolina. Within hours of Timothy McVeigh's arrival at Camp McCall, McVeigh told me he received a shock that altered the course of his life forever. As instructed, he had returned from the Persian Gulf and reported to Special Forces training in early April of 1991. The Army's Special Forces Training Complex at Camp McCall has an impressive history. In his mind, McVeigh knew he possessed "the talent, the guts, the brains and the balls" to become one of the Army's elite soldiers.

To his surprise, however, he was escorted into a windowless office in an administration building and told to wait. Within a few minutes, in walked a man McVeigh already knew as "the Major" from McVeigh's Army hitch in Iraq, though McVeigh never said exactly how he knew the Major, and never would identify him by name. McVeigh told me he found it strange that the Major was attired in civilian clothing and appeared unkempt by military standards. Unsure of exactly what to do, McVeigh stood and saluted the man.

After they exchanged greetings and touched on the state of affairs in Iraq, the reason for the meeting became clear. According to McVeigh, he and the Major were "close associates or borderline friends." This was true despite differences in their ages and ranks. They shared similar interests and had spoken often about many issues. The Major was a man McVeigh respected and sought to emulate.

In short order the Major launched into a slick and polished presentation about how difficult it was to find young leaders with enough intelligence, strength and loyalty to follow orders, conduct actions and campaigns without questioning the "why of things."

While leafing through McVeigh's personnel file and continuing to pump his ego by extolling his many admirable attributes, the Major had McVeigh's complete attention. He admitted to me the performance was "dazzling," especially when the Major worked in personal information from the file to supplement the accolades.

The Major reminded McVeigh that he had signed the Special Forces Assessment and Selection Statements of Understanding, and the Honor System, and inquired as to McVeigh's understanding of these documents. Then the Major confided that he now worked on "black-ops" projects, off the books. He invited McVeigh to work with him, and reluctantly revealed that his unit was attached to the Defense Department. According to the Major, the unit was so secret that even the Defense Secretary was unaware of its existence. The Major further explained that the agenda for this secret unit was primarily domestic intelligence gathering and internal threat evaluations with an emphasis on direct counter-action operations.

The Major stressed that if McVeigh agreed to sign on, he would be required to sign another confidentiality agreement never to disclose any information about the unit or its work. McVeigh's assignments would call for him to act separately from any other agents in the unit, relying on recruits or players of his own choosing when needed. Funding and support for the operations would be provided through sources unconnected to the U.S. government. McVeigh would be an agent acting alone, utilizing his own resourcefulness.

With his mind racing, McVeigh, ever the soldier boy with a burning desire to prove his worth, accepted on the spot. According to McVeigh, the Major told him to withdraw from Special Forces training, tone down his "hot-shot" performance in the Army and muster out by the end of the year.

In the meantime, McVeigh was to familiarize himself with the rhetoric of the extreme right-wing ideology and create the plausible aura of a disgruntled soldier. The Major instructed McVeigh to await further orders.

According to an FBI interview statement dated December 7, 1996, the Army provided the original documents relating to McVeigh's Special Forces training. These documents demonstrate that McVeigh entered the Special Forces on April 3, 1991, and then voluntarily withdrew from the training program four days later on April 7, when he signed his Voluntary Withdrawal Statement from the Special Forces Assessment and Selection Course. It is undisputed that McVeigh left the Special Forces within days of arriving at Camp McCall. However, his military medical records indicate he was given a medical examination at the Physician Exam Center at Irwin Army Community Hospital in Ft. Riley, Kansas, four months later, on August 22, 1991, at the request of two physicians – and that he was "qualified for Special Forces."

By December 1991, McVeigh had mustered out of the Army as an active duty soldier, but joined the National Guard Army Reserves in Buffalo, New York. He enlisted with the National Guard on November 13, 1991. He was then living with his father, William E. McVeigh, in Lockport, New York. McVeigh assumed the role of an ordinary civilian, but he was actually a sleeper agent now, part of the Major's black-op domestic surveillance unit. According to a Defense Department record, McVeigh held a DOD Secret Clearance that did not expire until May 11, 1995.

Agent McVeigh now immersed himself in research for his mission. His motivation was the Major's grim portrait – which McVeigh could still recite word for word – of a "country ripped apart by the militant movement, in specific, rogue elements, giving grass-roots Second Amendment advocates and your run of the mill tax protesters a bad name." According to the Major: "These groups are even more dangerous than armed criminals because they are on a mission with a defined ideology and creed, fueled by religious convictions."

One such domestic terrorist group that McVeigh already knew about was Robert Matthews' The Order, which was reported to have raised millions of dollars in robberies and carried out assassinations. McVeigh also familiarized himself with the history of James Ellison's Covenant, Sword and Arm of the Lord, a militia-style survivalist group in Northern Arkansas whose members are alleged to have committed murders and bombings. These activities landed one CSA captain on Arkansas' death row, where he was eventually executed the very same day as the Oklahoma City Bombing. Most of the group's other members ended up dead or imprisoned.

But as far as the world knew, Timothy McVeigh was just another Gulf War soldier who had come home to pick up his civilian life. For 14 months beginning in December 1991, McVeigh's official residence was in upstate New York, where he worked as a security guard. According to McVeigh, however, he oftentimes traveled to other areas beginning in early 1992, preparing for his new mission.

McVeigh was anxious to proceed with the assignment awaiting him. Working as a security guard and attending monthly National Guard weekends didn't hold his interest, though it did help support him. McVeigh's job with Burns International Security Services, Buffalo District, found him working as a rent-a-cop in an unarmed position. McVeigh claimed that while working for Burns Security he earned $7 an hour in 1991-92, more than his co-workers and some supervisors, who earned a maximum of $6.50 an hour. McVeigh took comfort in this claim, stating: "My boss would have me sneak in and get my check from her office." Eventually McVeigh obtained a position as an armed security guard, working for CALSPAN, which contracted with Burns Security. Nevertheless, most of his duties were routine. To McVeigh, this was a complete waste of his talents. "I felt lost and adrift while back in New York," he told me.

In a letter dated May 1, 1992, on Burns International Security stationery, McVeigh's employer stated:

> This communication is being sent to confirm that Timothy James McVeigh (an employee of Burns International Security) has recently been promoted to a supervisory position . . . Supervisor McVeigh's Army National Guard drills interfere greatly with his ability to perform this specific job. As we understand that Sergeant McVeigh has requested to be released from his commitment with the NYARNG, we only hope that you will grant him this reprieve.

The letter is signed by Linda McDonnell, Operations Manager. According to McVeigh's military records, he was honorably discharged from the Army National Guard after five months and one day of service on a four-year contractual agreement that was scheduled to end on May 11, 1996. At the time of discharge McVeigh continued to have a Top Security clearance. His rank was that of an E-5 Sergeant. His Separation and Discharge papers were signed by Charles M. Amoroso, Assistant Adjutant General, NYARNG.

All of this does not prove McVeigh's secret agent status, but it does raise questions as to whether his employment history during this period might actually have been a cover story.

By the summer days of August 1992, McVeigh was well on his way to becoming one of the anti-government zealots he was supposed to impersonate, or so it seemed. Depending upon which version one believes, he was for real, or he was acting. He wavered on this position when recounting his reaction to the August 21, 1992, raid by federal agents on the cabin of Randy Weaver in Ruby Ridge, Idaho. The raid followed a long standoff, after Weaver refused to surrender to authorities to face federal gun charges.

In the first few hours of that raid, Weaver's 14-year-old son was killed. Weaver's wife was shot and killed the next day. One deputy U.S. marshal was also killed in the gun battle. The Ruby Ridge standoff lasted 11 days before Randy Weaver surrendered.

During the siege at Ruby Ridge, McVeigh received a phone call from the Major. In a very brief exchange, the Major directed McVeigh to a meeting at Niagara Falls, New York, set for the following day. The meeting was short and to the point. McVeigh described the Major as being in an angry mood. As McVeigh recalled, the Major said: The "Ruby Ridge fiasco was a real cluster fuck for federal law enforcement" and that the militant movement would use the deaths of a woman and child as a rallying call to all like-minded Americans. The Major told McVeigh to heed that call. He was provided with a secure telephone number where he could leave messages for the Major.

McVeigh's mission was simple: he was to become a spy. In the words of his recruiter: "The survivalist and militia malcontents can destroy this country. It is up to you to prevent that from happening." The Major gave McVeigh $10,000 in used U.S. currency and told him to "put these funds to good use." According to McVeigh's bank records from the Federal Credit Union in Lockport, New York, where he maintained an account for several years, he made a deposit of $7,172.93 on September 28, 1992.

During the remaining months of 1992, McVeigh continued with his indoctrination into the anti-government agenda. He cultivated sources by mail and telephone. He also traveled some and attended meetings where skinheads gathered in Pennsylvania. McVeigh's father grew concerned over the noticeable changes in his son's behavior and attitude, and over his criticism of the government.

In mid-January, 1993, McVeigh received the telephone call he had been anxiously awaiting. The Major told him to wrap up his affairs and prepare for "months in the field." McVeigh was given an address in New Jersey and told to be there on a certain date and time.

At the appointed time McVeigh arrived in Vineland, New Jersey. As he pulled into the driveway of a small house in a rundown, predominantly Puerto Rican neighborhood, a dark complexioned man met him. The man appeared to speak fluent Spanish as he conversed with two children. Once inside, the swarthy man introduced himself as "Roberto," a friend of the Major.

McVeigh was provided with a stack of files and told to familiarize himself with the contents. These detailed dossiers contained information on well-known and obscure figures from various militant groups throughout the United States. Having spent endless hours reading books, reports and pamphlets in advance of this mission, he was amazed at the wealth of facts and figures he now had before him.

Agent McVeigh spent the next few days cloistered inside the house in a marathon of briefings. He listened to the odd-sounding accent of Roberto as he quizzed McVeigh thoroughly on the subjects and procedures contained in the documents. Contact with the Major, or any other agent from the unit, would be infrequent and only when absolutely necessary. All field reports were to be filed via voice recordings. To engage the system, a call would be placed to a telephone number McVeigh had to memorize. Once the connection was made the line was automatically secured and all verbal reports were encrypted as they were recorded. Only certain individuals, such as the Major, could access the reports and ascertain the identity of the agent making the report.

After three days McVeigh left Vineland with nothing except an envelope full of well used currency totaling $50,000. His instructions were to "immerse, inform on, and assess the actions of those in the right-wing, anti-government movement in the United States."

McVeigh used some of the funds to purchase merchandise such as T-shirts with "White Power" emblazoned on them, flags, books, uniforms and copies of the *Turner Diaries*, a book depicting the bombing of a government building. The flags were mostly Rebel flags. He assumed his role and was off to the gun show circuit where he would display his wares and blend in.

In January 1993, McVeigh arrived in Florida, where he set up shop at a gun show being held in the armory on State Highway 84 in Fort Lauderdale. He had visited his sister in Hollywood, and accepted a temporary job working with his brother-in-law for an electrical contractor. While at the gun show, McVeigh wore his Desert Storm uniform. He told me this helped in starting up conversations, and created a sense of trust with gun-show visitors. In uniform he came across as a patriot who cared for his country.

This Florida gun show was the beginning of McVeigh's undercover travels. Over the next two years and four months, leading up to the Oklahoma City Bombing, he would criss-cross the country, following the gun-show circuit. McVeigh found this environment to be perfect ground for networking with individuals who could further his mission. He was quickly able to establish a persona as a veteran with some extreme views. He often quoted the cadence from his boot camp training as inspiration: "Blood makes the grass grow. Kill, kill, kill!"

At the Fort Lauderdale show, McVeigh met Arkansas gun dealer Roger Moore. This would be the first of many contacts between the two men. Moore operated two businesses with his girlfriend Karen Anderson. They operated the American Assault Company and the Candy Store. Moore had residences in Pompano, Florida, and Royal, Arkansas. His presence on the gun show circuit was more of a hobby than anything else. He didn't need the money, as he had earned a considerable fortune when he sold a group of successful boat-building businesses.

Moore first noticed the clean-cut man dressed in his Desert Storm uniform as McVeigh stood behind a table selling merchandise. They struck up a conversation, and McVeigh introduced himself. According to an FBI interview statement, Moore claimed to have purchased a clock and Rebel flag from McVeigh during their first encounter. McVeigh told me they discussed the Second Amendment, the New World Order, the world money supply, white power and *The Turner Diaries*. McVeigh offered to share his table with Moore at an upcoming gun show at Dinner Key, in Coconut Grove, Florida. McVeigh had already reserved a table there and Moore hadn't. It was agreed they would meet there in four weeks.

McVeigh and Moore both attended the Dinner Key gun show and sold their wares from the same table. Moore seemed surprised that McVeigh was such a decent young man, and invited McVeigh to visit him at his ranch in Royal, Arkansas, after learning that McVeigh would be traveling west to attend the gun show in Tulsa, Oklahoma, in April.

The month of March 1993 found McVeigh near Waco, Texas, visiting the area surrounding the Mount Carmel compound that housed the religious group known as the Branch Davidians. On February 28, just the month before, federal law enforcement agents had raided the compound for the stated purpose of serving a search warrant. A fierce gun battle erupted, and several federal agents were killed or wounded. A 50-day standoff began. The siege at Waco galvanized the anti-government movement. For McVeigh, his presence on scene provided him with the perfect opportunity to improve his cover for the mission. He was fascinated by the media attention being given to the situation. He was interviewed as a spectator. This allowed him to use the knowledge he had accumulated and to memorialize his appearance at Waco.

McVeigh left Waco, traveling west to Arizona. In Kingman, he reunited with his old Army buddy Michael Fortier. During their time in the Army they spent many hours discussing and debating their beliefs on politically charged issues. In a letter from McVeigh to his sister Jennifer while he and Fortier were roommates, McVeigh tells her that: "We're quiet [sic] a team." He enclosed a picture of Fortier and told Jennifer to write to Fortier. That letter was dated March 12, 1990. Even more revealing is McVeigh's explanation to his defense team of the relationship he had with Fortier. In a memo dated May 30, 1996, written by Richard Burr, McVeigh explains that he developed a close relation with Fortier because: "when one is in the field, there's a buddy system, and that it is necessary for you to be there for your buddy."

According to Burr, "Mike Fortier was Tim's buddy." Mike knew the job, the concepts, and was McVeigh's "intellectual and physical equal." McVeigh described Fortier and himself as "birds of a feather." This undoubtedly figured in McVeigh's decision to recruit his old friend for his new mission. McVeigh told me more than once that he knew that he could trust Mike with his life. McVeigh's visit was brief. Fortier had a live-in girlfriend named Lori. McVeigh found that he was experiencing some jealousy, but he insisted: "When I say jealousy, I don't mean in a perverted way. It's not a sexual thing. I was just emotionally involved and that took away from the bond we shared before I shipped off to the Gulf War. I sort of felt like a third wheel."

McVeigh had found the gun show circuit to be fertile ground as he sought to infiltrate the anti-government Patriot movement. Having long possessed an interest in weapons and the Second Amendment, McVeigh felt at home amongst the gun show crowd. It didn't take long for him to become a fixture at gun shows across the country. He found an in with many younger people involved in skinhead groups and the white power crowd. During this period everyone was talking about the siege at Waco, and guessing what action the government would take to end it.

In April 1993, McVeigh attended the event in Tulsa that billed itself as the "World's Largest Gun Show." McVeigh listened, learned and observed. He didn't have a booth at this event, but he met up with Roger Moore and Karen Anderson. As McVeigh made his way from booth to booth, having many conversations, he was surprised by just how much he had in common with these folks on whom he was spying. Their interest in guns and maintaining the right to own them, while remaining free from government interference, seemed perfectly logical. He told me he asked himself: "Can these people really be a legitimate threat to this country?"

At the conclusion of the Tulsa gun show, McVeigh followed Roger Moore and Karen Anderson to their Arkansas ranch. McVeigh intended to stay several weeks. In their FBI interview statements, Moore and Anderson said they were somewhat irritated when McVeigh just "took over the house." Moore and Anderson reported that McVeigh kept going into the kitchen and fixing his own meals, eating whatever he wanted to, spent most of his time reading magazines such as *Time, U.S. News and World Report, Soldier of Fortune, Firearms Journal, NRA Magazine,* and *Travel Magazine.* According to Anderson, McVeigh seemed "antsy" and "hyper" when discussing what he was reading. During his short stay of less than three days he assisted Anderson with various odd jobs. He did so over Moore's objections that Anderson shouldn't be putting their houseguest to work. McVeigh grew angry over Moore's statements and left shortly afterwards.

McVeigh had been impressed with Moore's ranch. He described the area as being "laid back." Unbeknownst to the gun dealers, Moore and Anderson were being observed and befriended by an agent of the U.S. government intent on harming the Patriot movement.

On April 19, 1993, McVeigh was visiting the family farm of his friend and ex-platoon leader Terry Nichols in Decker, Michigan. Nichols lived with his wife Marife and her toddler son Jason, along with Nichols' brother James. They shared the farmhouse where McVeigh became a frequent visitor.

On this day McVeigh and the others watched in horror as the Branch Davidian compound in Waco burned to the ground, live on national television. The fire began after government agents attacked the Davidians with a tank. The structures appeared to ignite, and the fire spread immediately. All of the Davidians inside perished: men, women and children alike – at least 71 total, with 17 being children.

McVeigh immediately drove to a nearby pay phone and tried to contact the Major. While watching news coverage of the carnage at Waco, McVeigh had caught a glimpse of the Major in the background of a television interview. McVeigh told me he wondered: What was the Major's involvement in Waco? After three days he finally reached his secret unit. The Major was, however, unavailable. Somewhat dazed and confused, McVeigh felt compelled to reassess his current mission. So far he had done nothing more than pass along weekly reports on various individuals he'd met at gun shows and meetings. Was Waco one of the actions contemplated by the Major when he recruited McVeigh into the unit? This question played over and over in McVeigh's mind.

After the Waco raid McVeigh was restless and soon departed Michigan. He was on the road for several days. He traveled through Indiana, Illinois, Missouri and Oklahoma, where he met with a German national named Andreas Carl Strassmeir at a motel in Muskogee, Oklahoma. Strassmeir plays a key role in McVeigh's account of the bomb plot. McVeigh had first met Strassmeir, whom he called "Andy the German" and, at times, "Andy the Kraut" at the Tulsa gun show several weeks earlier. Strassmeir was the firearms and paramilitary arms trainer at Elohim City, a Christian Identity religious community in rural Adair County in eastern Oklahoma. According to a McVeigh defense memo dated December 27, 1995, McVeigh admitted meeting Strassmeir and two of his companions at the Tulsa gun show and discussing Waco. Strassmeir also admitted in a sworn declaration to meeting McVeigh at the Tulsa gun show "two years before the Oklahoma City Bombing."

In the meeting with Strassmeir at the Muskogee motel, McVeigh tried to assess the mood in the Patriot movement following the Waco raid. Strassmeir told McVeigh that many Patriots were intent on some type of a response against the federal government, which they held directly responsible for the deaths of the Branch Davidians. In the meeting, McVeigh expressed sympathy for that position, partly because he believed it would enhance his cover, but partly because he was genuinely upset over the deaths of the children and others at Waco, or so he told me.

According to McVeigh, Strassmeir and the other residents of Elohim City were fearful of a Waco type raid on their own community. Strassmeir invited McVeigh to visit Elohim City, which McVeigh said he did, several months later. He said Strassmeir and others knew him at Elohim City by the name "Tim Tuttle," one of McVeigh's aliases.

In May 1993, the Major instructed McVeigh to begin organizing a group of men in the Patriot movement who would be willing to undertake a military style action when the time was right.

McVeigh had returned to Kingman, and worked for a while as a security guard at State Security. He was staying with Mike Fortier. It is during this time Tim said he first used drugs, including marijuana, which he stated, "made me depressed and made me cry," and crystal methadrine, which "made me feel I had the answers to the universe." McVeigh also had his own place in Kingman for several months. He resigned his position at State Security in July 1993.

In a letter from McVeigh to his longtime friend Steve Hodge dated July 30, McVeigh wrote: "The time for playing games is over. This

Deadly Secrets

communication is too important to send through the regular channels; it comes direct to you from me." He also forwarded a copy of a video concerning Waco and asked that Hodge's whole family watch it. In the letter, McVeigh alleges lies told by the government during the Waco cover-up, and asks Hodge to consider evidence that the federal Bureau of Alcohol, Tobacco and Firearms murdered the Branch Davidians. McVeigh concludes the letter by saying: "Jesus, man, wake up!!!"

McVeigh told me that during the summer of 1993, he traveled to several U.S. military bases where he had access via his Defense Department Secret Clearance designation. He claimed to have toured the facilities and engaged in maneuvers with troops at U.S. Army bases. Some of these included Camp Grafton, North Dakota; Fort Sill, Oklahoma; and Fort Riley, Kansas. His real reason for these visits was to scout armories and determine the possibility of obtaining large destructive weapons "by whatever means necessary." When pressed on this, McVeigh was vague at first, but later claimed: "I knew a big mission was coming, and the Major had instructed me to scout Army bases with some others from the unit. We knew that explosives would be needed, and a base is the best place to find those."

In September, McVeigh attended the *Soldier of Fortune* gun show in Las Vegas. This is the largest gun show in the country and was held at The Sands hotel. McVeigh met up with Roger Moore, also know as Robert or Bob Miller. Moore claimed that he became upset with McVeigh because of his discussions with someone at the gun show with a law enforcement badge under his coat. McVeigh was debating Patriot-related activities that Moore thought would attract unneeded attention to him as McVeigh was working Moore's booth. When Moore voiced his concerns, McVeigh became angry and stomped off.

During this convention in Las Vegas, McVeigh had a face-to-face meeting with the Major. They had in-depth conversations regarding some of the individuals McVeigh had met and established contact with. Now the Major instructed McVeigh to form a strike team to carry out a domestic bombing. Up until this point, McVeigh's mission had only been gathering intelligence and establishing contacts. The Major assured McVeigh that he, the Major, had not been involved in the events at Waco other than as an observer. McVeigh told me: "I knew that he was lying through his teeth, just like he lied about Ruby Ridge."

The Major supplied McVeigh with another infusion of cash and revealed the timetable for the mission. The Major's prior orders had been cryptic. Now, all of that had changed. He provided McVeigh with a specific course of action, and McVeigh now knew exactly what was expected of him. The bombing would put an end to the growing strength of the Patriot, militia and survivalist movements. Some in the federal government, including the Major, saw that fringe element of America as "one of the largest threats to ever face this nation."

McVeigh sent out an SOS to many of his contacts. He whittled down their varied responses and asked several to meet him in the rural encampment of Elohim City. He was ready to gather his team and begin preparing them for the mission.

After leaving Las Vegas, McVeigh traveled to Kansas with several stops along the way, including one in Grand Junction, Colorado, on the western slope of the Rocky Mountains. Here he visited Executive Security International. This private school provides training in executive protection, investigation and intelligence operations, including anti-terrorism. Some of McVeigh's former colleagues from the first Gulf War were associated with ESI.

During the first week of October 1993, McVeigh and Terry Nichols attended a gun show in Knob Creek, Kentucky. McVeigh told me that he spoke with numerous individuals who were experts in the field of explosives at this gun show. He obtained a copy of a book titled *The Ranger Handbook* that he said was very useful to him while planning and preparing for the bombing. He also met up with Roger Moore and Karen Anderson at the Knob Creek event.

McVeigh and Nichols traveled to Fayetteville, Arkansas, where they searched for property to purchase. Motel records from a Motel 6 in Fayetteville show that Nichols registered there on October 11 and 12, 1993. They drove from Fayetteville to Elohim City, which is near the Arkansas/Oklahoma state line. McVeigh was issued a traffic ticket in Crawford County, Arkansas, approximately five miles from the Oklahoma state line on October 12 while en route to Elohim City.

McVeigh had previously met Rev. Mark Thomas, a racist preaching anti-government zealot who operated from his farm near Allentown, Pennsylvania. McVeigh had attended a weekend rally there while waiting to be called upon by the Major. Rev. Thomas was popular amongst some skinhead groups in the area. He was also a longtime friend and associate of Rev. Robert G. Millar, the leader and patriarch of Elohim City. With assistance from Mark Thomas and Andreas Strassmeir, McVeigh was able to arrange the meeting at Elohim City, and ensure his recruits were on hand.

While at Elohim City, McVeigh, Nichols and others who had come for the meeting toured the compound and fired their weapons on the practice range. Strassmeir served as firearms instructor and paramilitary trainer at the request of Rev. Millar.

According to McVeigh, those in attendance at the October 1993 meeting included Nichols, Strassmeir, and Dennis Mahon, the Oklahoma chapter leader of the White Aryan Resistance, and a former Grand Imperial Dragon of the KKK. Also at the meeting were members of a bank robbery gang with extreme anti-government politics, who will play a central role in McVeigh's account of the bombing. Those present at the meeting included Richard Guthrie, Peter Langan, Shawn Kenny and Kevin McCarthy.

Guthrie and Langan were co-leaders of the bank-robbery gang. Guthrie was a small-time criminal with a history of violence, hatred for the U.S. government and having made threats against President George H.W. Bush. McVeigh had first met Guthrie through Mark Thomas while in Pennsylvania.

Peter Langan was unknown to McVeigh prior to the meeting at Elohim City. Strassmeir and Guthrie vouched for Langan, as they did for several others McVeigh recruited. McVeigh told me he preferred men who were not easily recognizable to law enforcement and who could blend in where needed.

McVeigh and Strassmeir emerged as the group's leaders in the meeting. The group committed to a mission: a direct strike against the federal government in retaliation for the raids on Ruby Ridge and Waco. According to McVeigh, they envisioned "an eye for an eye" type attack. "I wanted to plant a seed," he told me. "A specific mission would be developed, but for now it was enough that we had agreed to raise money to fund the attack. We would select a suitable soft target, plan, and then act."

Within a matter of months after the Elohim City meeting, McVeigh told me that he, Langan and Guthrie were robbing banks in order to fund the mission. McVeigh's involvement with Guthrie, Langan and their gang has long been speculated upon, and evidence does exist that the FBI investigated McVeigh's involvement in planning the robberies, and his actual participation as a getaway driver. But publicly, at least, the FBI has discounted any link between McVeigh and the bank robberies. And most curiously, government prosecutors were silent about the robberies – believed to have netted as much as a quarter of a million dollars – when they made their bombing case against McVeigh and Nichols.

The subject of the bank robberies and their connection to McVeigh's undercover mission came up in letters McVeigh wrote his sister Jennifer soon after the Elohim City meeting in late 1993. In letters dated October 20 and December 24, 1993, McVeigh wrote that he was associated with a group of people who shared similar beliefs as his own. The letters go into detail about his having been recruited during Special Forces training because he was one of 10 out of 400 who scored the highest in certain test areas. McVeigh said his group would be helping the CIA bring drugs into the U.S., and they would work hand in hand with police agencies to quiet those who were security risks. The December letter stated that McVeigh was on the move again. He acknowledged associating with "our friends who knock over banks." He characterized the endeavor as a sort of Robin Hood situation in which the government is the evil king. "We are at war with the system . . .we have to fund our war efforts with, sometimes, covert means," McVeigh wrote.

McVeigh told me that he was leaving a paper trail by design. "I was following orders," he said. " It had to be known that I hated the government. Even my own family had to believe my cover. Otherwise I could have ended up dead before the mission was completed."

On November 22, 1993, McVeigh was in Michigan, visiting the Nichols' family farm. On that day, Terry Nichols' son was found dead. The official report states that the toddler's death was accidental. Apparently the boy smothered himself with plastic. McVeigh and Nichols tried to revive him. They performed CPR on the small body. An ambulance crew came and transported little Jason to a nearby hospital where he was pronounced dead. McVeigh provided some contradictory information to others and me about this incident.

At one point, when recounting the events surrounding Jason's death, McVeigh admitted that he had actually killed the boy because of his anger at Nichols' wife, Marife, after she rebuffed his sexual advances. McVeigh first mentioned this in response to a question about the children who had been killed in the Oklahoma City Bombing. He said: "It's not hard to kill children, after already having killed one." This was a stunning response, and when I followed up on it, McVeigh confessed to having smothered Jason Nichols.

At a different time, McVeigh was adamant that he had only been joking, that he had actually been dismayed to learn that Marife believed he had killed her little boy. Tim was angry and visibly moved when discussing the incident. He said: "The fuckin' bitch suspected me of killin' that half-breed kid. If anyone wanted to kill him, it would have been Terry. He knew that kid wasn't even his." Actually, while Jason Nichols wasn't Terry's biological son, he wasn't half of any race. Both his mother and father were Filipino. McVeigh was visibly agitated when talking about Jason Nichols' death. His body movements, hand gestures and animated speech patterns were pronounced.

During the investigation by local law enforcement of Jason's death, McVeigh made the mistake of identifying himself as Tim Tuttle, and only later as Tim McVeigh. This misstep was a learning experience for McVeigh. He had brought unwanted scrutiny upon himself. Being investigated, even briefly, by the local Michigan cops wasn't on his agenda. Some fast-talking on his part convinced the local officer that his use of an alias was not sinister and had nothing to do with the child's death. According to some who attended McVeigh's federal trial in Denver, the officer stated that he always suspected McVeigh of having some involvement in Jason Nichols' death.

McVeigh's involvement with Peter Langan and Richard Guthrie progressed from a talking stage to action in January 1994. During meetings the trio planned strategies for robbing banks and armored cars. McVeigh's inside knowledge from having worked as an armed security guard was invaluable as he provided his partners with information. He saw his partnership with these men, willing to act in conjunction with him to help finance the overthrow of the federal government, as God sent. McVeigh was well on his way to infiltrating militant groups and raising money that could not be traced: exactly the objective the Major had given him.

According to McVeigh's accounts, he helped to "plan, case and rob banks" with Langan and Guthrie, beginning with banks in Iowa. He used the gun show circuit as his cover, and personally drove getaway cars during some of the heists. This band of brothers would take on new members, expand and become known as the Aryan Republican Army in the months to follow. The media dubbed the gang the Midwest Bank Bandits.

One of McVeigh's contacts included a skinhead named David Lynch from Port Saint Lucie, Florida, whom McVeigh met at a gun show in the area. According to Klanwatch, published by the Southern Poverty Law Center, an advocacy group against hate crimes and white supremacy, Lynch was a leader of the white supremacist group, American Front, and had connections to methamphetamine dealers. Skinheads usually do not use drugs, but McVeigh claimed that Lynch had a network of skinhead dealers and others in the Patriot movement.

McVeigh's use of crystal meth, a potent form of speed, is well documented. His sources for this drug were not limited to the suppliers known to him and the Fortiers in Kingman, as some have speculated. While McVeigh and the Fortiers did purchase regularly from a dealer named James Rosencrans in Kingman, McVeigh formed a loose association with Lynch that benefited them both. McVeigh told me that his use of meth was far more than recreational. "I needed it in order to fulfill my mission," he said. "The U.S. military regularly issues speed to its pilots and Special Forces who are required to be awake and on duty for hours and even days at a time."

McVeigh's need to justify his drug use seemed very important to him. When quizzed on this, he said: "I'm not like the ghetto dwelling crackhead porch monkeys you find in every prison in this country or on the streets of every fuckin' city around, and I don't wanna be lumped into the same category as those jungle bunnies. I saw plenty of that during my rounds in Buffalo."

McVeigh's first experience with meth was with Michael Fortier. McVeigh claimed it allowed him to explore thoughts, ideas and to plan in ways that motivated him. The drug was an additional tool or weapon in his arsenal.

Having embarked upon a quasi-criminal career, McVeigh wanted to ensure that his superiors in the unit officially sanctioned his position. The Major had provided him with assurances and a telephone number to call if he were ever arrested. At some point, he received a law enforcement badge that he carried in his wallet. According to an FBI interview statement from the Oklahoma City Bombing case, McVeigh had a law enforcement badge in his wallet at the time of his arrest.

However, the badge presented a potential problem. McVeigh didn't want anyone in the criminal world, the Patriot/militia movement, or those on the gun show circuit to perceive him as a government agent or cop. So he took to showing the badge as a prank, as if it was a realistic-looking replica of a real badge. Ironically, he and the ARA bank robbery crew began using other law enforcement paraphernalia, such as FBI and ATF windbreakers and jackets. The group also used police radios and scanners to monitor local police and federal law enforcement frequencies while planning and conducting criminal operations. McVeigh stated: "Everyone was impressed when I was able to secure the radio frequencies for the FBI and ATF." The Major provided these to him.

Between February and July of 1994, McVeigh lived a nomadic lifestyle while based in Kingman, Arizona. Some 19 trips out of Arizona in 1994 took him to Kansas, Michigan and New York, but he never stayed in any one place for long. McVeigh continued to travel the gun show circuit, had secret meetings with Patriots, militia members and the ARA. He participated in bank robberies and reported faithfully to the Major. He was able to purchase materials for making small pipe bombs. He was learning more and more about explosives on his own.

In a letter to his sister dated March 23, 1994, and postmarked Las Vegas, McVeigh wrote that he had worn himself ragged running, so he was settling in one spot. He said: "Being as it's been more than two years since I got out, things may be O.K. now." He also told her that if anyone unusual came looking for him in New York she should immediately call Mike and Lori Fortier's phone number. He also asked his sister if she was posing naked.

In Roger Moore's May 19, 1995, FBI interview statement, he claimed McVeigh came unannounced to his ranch in Royal, Arkansas, in late April 1994. This was McVeigh's third trip to the ranch. He had also visited in early 1994, while Karen Anderson was there alone. Moore said he observed a noticeable change in McVeigh on this visit. He wanted to sleep where he could look out the window to see if anyone was approaching the residence. He slept with a gun under his pillow. McVeigh normally had in his possession a .45 caliber handgun, but on this occasion he had added a mini 30 Ruger. After two days McVeigh left abruptly. Moore did not remember any argument or altercation between himself and McVeigh. About a month later, Moore received a letter from McVeigh advising him that he was back in Kingman, and providing contact information.

It appears that McVeigh was becoming paranoid and was fearful for his own safety. When I questioned him about this he seemed to shrug it off and became defensive and wanted to change the subject. At one point he did admit, "I was always searching, didn't know who I could trust. I tested everyone, even my own blood."

During this period McVeigh and the ARA bank bandits used fake bombs during their robberies. This ruse was designed to confuse cops and delay organized investigations while the robbers escaped the area.

McVeigh's travels took him all across the United States, and money provided by the Major was his main source of support. McVeigh told me his proceeds from the bank robberies were minimal. His forays into working short terms at legitimate jobs or ventures brought in only meager sums of money. He certainly didn't earn enough from his gun show sales to support himself and his travels. There absolutely wasn't enough income to purchase the items required to build a truck bomb.

April 1994: McVeigh was once again in Tulsa for a gun show. He had a lengthy meeting with Andreas Strassmeir and Dennis Mahon. During this meeting, specific targets for a bombing were first discussed. The first choice was the Alfred P. Murrah Federal Building in Oklahoma City. Other possible targets included the Federal Courthouse in Fort Smith, Arkansas, the Tulsa Federal Building or IRS office.

The choice of the Murrah Federal Building in Oklahoma City intrigued McVeigh because during the 1980s it had been the potential target of a bombing planned by members of the Covenant, Sword and Arm of the Lord. Additionally, the Murrah Building also housed some federal law enforcement agencies. That was appealing in its own way. He had much to ponder, but a deciding factor would be just how accessible and "soft" the target was.

Andreas Strassmeir

Dennis Mahon

A decision was made to assess the choices. McVeigh, Strassmeir and others would do this personally in the unit. It was also decided that supplies or explosives for making a bomb would need to be stockpiled. McVeigh volunteered to undertake the task of obtaining and storing the supplies. At Mahon's insistence it was agreed that Mark Thomas and "his students" – including Michael Brescia, Kevin McCarthy and Scott Stedeford – would assist in the mission.

Strassmeir and McVeigh spoke about their mutual friends Roger Moore and Karen Anderson as a potential source for explosives needed to build a bomb. Moore had access to explosives through their business, the American Assault Company. Both McVeigh and Nichols would later claim that Roger Moore did provide explosives to be used in the Oklahoma City Bombing. McVeigh told me Karen Anderson had befriended McVeigh, Strassmeir, Richard Guthrie and Michael Brescia. McVeigh told me that Anderson had a penchant for younger men, and oftentimes entertained them with viewing pornographic videos that she and Moore sold under the counter via their business, the Candy Store. According to McVeigh, these men would visit Anderson in Arkansas while Moore was away or living in Florida.

On one of McVeigh's nomadic trips, sometime in 1994, he paid a visit to Terry Nichols, who was now living and working in Kansas. He and his wife Marife and their children lived in a small house in Herington while Nichols worked as a farmhand on a nearby ranch. This was the first of many such visits by McVeigh to Herington.

At about the same time, Pete Langan of the ARA, using an alias, rented a house in Pittsburgh, Kansas. The distance between the ARA safe house and Nichols' home was less than 150 miles. McVeigh's connection to both Nichols and the ARA safe house is something he bragged about when recounting just how stupid the federal agents were. "How could they miss that?" he asked. "My sister told the FBI that I'd been robbing banks, and Terry's bitch ex-wife told 'em he was involved with a group of bank robbers."

While back in Arizona, his home base in 1994, McVeigh continued to use crystal meth as a source of inspiration and to establish his bond with a group of meth dealers in and around Kingman. The Fortiers had introduced him to their main dealer, but McVeigh didn't trust him. That mistrust was well placed because James Rosencrans, the dealer in question, was one of many witnesses who testified against McVeigh at his trial. According to McVeigh, he had purchased a "bulk load of meth" from Andreas Strassmeir in Elohim City. McVeigh kept a personal stash, but put the rest out for sale on consignment.

According to McVeigh, he placed some of this meth with Cheyne Kehoe, who lived in the Spokane area. McVeigh had met Kehoe at a gun show in Nevada. He was part of a Christian Identity family who were regulars at the Elohim City compound. McVeigh told me he had done meth with Kehoe, who was heavily into the drug. For that reason, McVeigh fronted Kehoe a shipment of crystal meth to sell. McVeigh saw in him a bright, young, intelligent potential warrior with a drive to succeed.

McVeigh shared his meth with some in the Kingman area, but he refused to sell it himself, and certainly not there. "I didn't want to step on any toes," he said. "You learn quick not to shit in your own backyard." He had come a long way from his "boy next door" image.

There was someone else in Kingman, who McVeigh told me played an important role in his plans to build a bomb. Karen Anderson and Roger Moore were acquaintances of one Steven Colbern, who had purchased ammunition and other items from them by mail, although they claim not to have met Colbern in person. Knowing that McVeigh and Colbern had much in common, and were both in the Kingman area, Anderson introduced McVeigh to Colbern. But at Roger Moore's insistence, Anderson introduced McVeigh as Tim Tuttle.

In short order, McVeigh and Colbern were camping in the desert and in caves, doing maneuvers, talking, sharing ideas and teaching one another. Colbern was by all accounts a paranoid man with various anti-government views. He had caches of food and supplies stashed in numerous locations awaiting a doomsday event. Colbern had a chemistry degree from the University of California at Los Angeles. McVeigh told me Colbern "was super intelligent, had lots of guts, and he knew plenty about explosives." They were both secretive personalities, and McVeigh seemed to light up and smile when recounting tales about his friendship with Colbern.

By summer's end, 1994, McVeigh pulled up stakes, packed his meager belongings and prepared to head east. Before his departure he said his goodbyes to Colbern, but only after obtaining specific information he needed for building a bomb. McVeigh now had in his pocket a completed list of the exact components needed for his bombing mission.

McVeigh explained to me how he, Mike Fortier, Colbern and others had designed, made and exploded several types of small bombs out in the desert during the spring and mid-summer of 1994. McVeigh once drew a diagram of a pipe bomb and a clock timer to demonstrate how easily a bomb could be constructed. "The device would kill a person if placed under the driver's seat of a car," he said. At one point McVeigh told me that his No. 1 choice for making explosive devices was his friend the chemist: Steve Colbern.

In August, after leaving Kingman and visiting Nichols in Kansas, McVeigh met up with Pete Langan at the annual motorcycle rally held in Sturgis, South Dakota. According to McVeigh, he and Langan spent several days at the rally, which attracts bikers and others by the thousands every year. They come from around the country and Canada to attend this event. McVeigh told me he and Langan spent time drinking, doing meth, and riding Pete's bike. At times McVeigh was riding behind Langan on what McVeigh termed the "bitch seat." McVeigh seemed pained when recalling the details. He had real problems with accepting the fact that he had formed a partnership with a "sexual deviant" after learning years later that Langan was a cross dresser and wanted to become a woman.

During the Sturgis rally, Langan and McVeigh had several discussions about the potential for robbing an armored car. Members of the ARA were intent on pursuing such a robbery. McVeigh's experience and employment with an armored car company provided the bank robbers with an insider's information. While McVeigh and Langan were in South Dakota, Richard Guthrie was back in Pennsylvania, but he had made a stop to see his old friend Shawn Kenny in Ohio before traveling on to Mark Thomas' farm near Allentown.

In September 1994, McVeigh arrived at Elohim City, where he once again met with Dennis Mahon and Andreas Strassmeir. At this meeting McVeigh met Michael Brescia for the first time. Brescia was Strassmeir's roommate and assistant at Elohim City – and the newest member of the Aryan Republican Army. McVeigh was impressed by

Brescia. "I liked him almost immediately," McVeigh said. "I could tell he had brains and guts."

McVeigh, Strassmeir and Mahon had decided on the Murrah Federal Building in Oklahoma City as the target for the bombing. This building was a symbolic target and had a history within the Patriot communities. The date for the mission was also decided - April 19, 1995 - the second anniversary of the Waco fire. Unbeknownst to those in attendance, however, their secret plan wasn't a secret to the federal government anymore. One month before, the Tulsa office of the Bureau of Alcohol, Tobacco and Firearms had opened an investigation into Mahon and WAR. Mahon's former girlfriend, Carol Howe, had become an ATF informant. In months to come, she would specifically inform her two handlers, David E. Roberts and case agent Angela Findley Graham, that Mahon and Strassmeir were casing federal buildings in Oklahoma with the idea of blowing them up. As of August 1994, then, almost a year before the bombing, the U.S. government began acquiring information through informant Carol Howe that Strassmeir and Mahon were targeting the Murrah Building from Elohim City.

After the meeting, McVeigh, Brescia and Mahon used the Elohim City gun range for target practice. "Mike B. was good, but I was better," McVeigh said, as he bragged about his marksmanship abilities.

Some have speculated that this September 1994 visit to Elohim City was McVeigh's first to the compound. I questioned him specifically about this. McVeigh was adamant, saying: "This was actually my fourth visit there. Fuckin' government rats don't know everything about me."

He was just as forceful when stating that Terry Nichols was not present at this particular meeting. Court records show that it was McVeigh who rented a room at a motel in Vian, Oklahoma, on September 12. Vian is only a short distance from Elohim City.

On September 21, McVeigh (also known as "Speedie"), told me he was the wheelman for a bank robbery in Overland Park, Kansas. He drove after ARA members Richard Guthrie and Pete Langan robbed the bank.

September 1994: According to the government's case against McVeigh and Nichols, this month marked the beginning of the conspiracy to bomb the Murrah Building. According to McVeigh's account, however, the plan had been operational for several months.

McVeigh was now focusing on acquiring explosives. In September, he said, he bought some stolen explosives from a speak freak. According to McVeigh, Roger Moore was the middleman in this deal. The speed freak contacted Moore as a potential buyer. Moore put McVeigh in contact with the man, and a deal was struck.

During September and October, McVeigh was on the move, traveling from west to east and back west again. He visited his mother, sister, grandfather, Roger Moore, and others. He and Terry Nichols obtained bomb-making supplies and rented the storage facilities to keep them in. McVeigh also claims he cased the Murrah Building with Nichols and later with Fortier. On October 4, McVeigh rented a storage space in his own name at the Northern Storage Company in Kingman. He used that space to store detonators and other items. Lori Fortier claimed it was on October 7 that McVeigh told her he had selected the Murrah Building as his target for the bombing.

On approximately October 20, 1994, McVeigh, Nichols, Guthrie, Strassmeir and Brescia met in Tulsa, Oklahoma. According to McVeigh, they were brought together at the request of Karen Anderson. It was simple: Anderson wanted Roger Moore killed. She wanted to contract with someone within the McVeigh group to commit the murder, but it had to be done soon. There is no record of any such meeting, but it has been confirmed that on October 21, Karen Anderson was at a Tulsa gun show selling merchandise for the American Assault Company. Richard Guthrie and Andreas Strassmeir were also present at the gun show. Court records and investigative reports show that McVeigh and Nichols were in Texas that day. But according to McVeigh, he and Nichols drove from Tulsa to Oklahoma City after the meeting with Anderson. Then, McVeigh said they cased the Murrah Building and traveled on to Texas.

McVeigh's account of the Tulsa meeting, which he told me was held in Anderson's motel room, made it clear that Anderson and Strassmeir had spoken previously about the contract. It was Strassmeir who had contacted McVeigh, Brescia and Guthrie at Anderson's request. Anderson said she wanted the job done on November 5, 1994. The verbal contract was accepted. It called for Moore to be murdered, and for the house to be robbed of cash, weapons, jewels, gold and silver. McVeigh said Anderson provided them with a set of keys to her Royal,

Arkansas, home and to the van belonging to Roger Moore. McVeigh said Anderson gave specific instructions that certain items belonging to her were not to be taken.

In late October, McVeigh began recruiting another prospective accomplice: Shawn Kenny, an ARA member who lived in and around Cincinnati, Ohio. They had first met in Elohim City several months earlier. Richard Guthrie and Pete Langan were close associates of Kenny's. He was a young man who reminded McVeigh of Mike Fortier and Cheyne Kehoe. McVeigh told me he had numerous conversations with Kenny about his plans to bomb the Murrah Building. He had grown to trust Kenny after their participation in a bank robbery. According to McVeigh, Kenny had assisted McVeigh in obtaining some explosives that he later used in the bombing. On November 4, 1994, Kenny agreed to assist McVeigh and the others in the Oklahoma City Bombing.

At around the same time, McVeigh first learned of his grandfather's death during a telephone call to Mike Fortier on October 21, 1994. McVeigh seemed very somber and reflective when discussing this with me. He left Kansas and drove east on his way back to Pendleton, New York. McVeigh told me he made stops in Miamitown, Ohio, for a meeting with Shawn Kenny and Columbus, where he was the wheelman for a bank robbery committed by Langan, Guthrie and Scott Stedeford, the newest addition to the Midwest Bank Bandits. The Columbus National Bank was believed to have been robbed on October 24 by three men, but actually there were four. McVeigh was never inside the bank, so witnesses saw only three robbers.

By early November 1994, McVeigh was in his hometown helping to dispose of his grandfather's estate. During the midst of his stay, he left New York for a quick trip to the Niles Gun Show in Akron, Ohio. On November 5, the day set for the Roger Moore contract, McVeigh was a guest at a motel in Kent, Ohio. According to McVeigh, he was at the gun show on November 5 and 6.

On November 5, Richard Guthrie and Mike Brescia robbed Roger Moore, according to McVeigh. They did so with ease. The robbery took approximately two hours. Moore always claimed to have seen only one robber. The robbery began when Moore was confronted by a shotgun-toting man who ordered Moore into his house where he was tied up. The robbery netted approximately $64,000 in items, including 77 guns,

Deadly Secrets

200-250 pieces of precious jewels, camera equipment and $17,650 in cash, silver and gold, according to the Farmer's Insurance report and adjuster Rick Spivey. The Garland County Sheriff's Department report differs slightly, indicating there was between $20,000 and $24,000 in cash, silver and gold taken. None of Karen Anderson's jewelry or property was taken during the robbery.

Roger Moore was left alive and unhurt. His hands were tied but left loose enough so that he was easily able to free himself and go to a neighbor's house to call for assistance. According to Mrs. Walt Powel, Moore was sporting a .45 pistol in his belt when he entered the Powel residence. Mrs. Powel also stated that Moore used the phone to call someone whom he spoke to in a low voice to report what had happened. Only after Mrs. Powel's son had arrived and retrieved her husband, who was working at a nearby church, were they able to coax Moore into contacting the sheriff's department to report the robbery.

According to McVeigh, it was Andreas Strassmeir's last minute decision to call off the hit on Moore, and go forward with the robbery only. McVeigh told me that Strassmeir had secretly recorded one of his conversations with Anderson and felt he was in control of the situation. McVeigh was livid at first over the change in plans. He feared that Roger Moore would suspect him of involvement in the robbery. That would be impossible if Moore was dead. In hindsight, though, McVeigh concluded it was good that Moore hadn't been killed.

McVeigh made sure to establish an ironclad alibi for the time of the crime. When explaining why he left New York for the gun show in Ohio to establish his alibi, he said: "I didn't want my family involved in my world. Even the cops don't believe family members when an alibi is involved. Records and strangers make a much stronger alibi."

The proceeds from the Moore robbery were eventually split, and part of the money found its way into financing the Oklahoma City Bombing. Strassmeir's decision to double-cross Anderson and to threaten her with blackmail was what McVeigh described as "a stroke of pure genius," because the robbery would likely be considered an inside job or a case of insurance fraud. The heat from a robbery/murder would have been intense. McVeigh claimed he took possession of most of the weapons from the Moore robbery, and that he and Fortier later sold them. As McVeigh told this part of his story, it was obvious to me that he had not been happy with Strassmeir acting on his own with the change in plans. It threatened McVeigh's sense of control. He couldn't trust Strassmeir.

On November 11, 1994, ARA members Langan and Guthrie, along with an unknown getaway driver, robbed a bank in Des Moines, Iowa. In discussing this robbery, McVeigh smiled and said: "The feds are like Keystone cops. They can't do shit unless they have some informant doing their job for them. I was all across the country doing these jobs. I'm the best wheelman around." He made this statement more than once, but we were discussing the Des Moines bank robbery this time. When I attempted to pin him down as to whether he was the wheelman for this particular robbery, he was evasive.

On December 3, 1994, McVeigh traveled to a gun show in Kalamazoo, Michigan. He had meetings with members of the Michigan Militia and with a Patriot in Three Rivers. He then traveled back to Ohio where he visited Shawn Kenny. McVeigh told me Kenny provided materials for establishing fake identities. The items included blank baptismal certificates, birth certificates, insurance cards and instructions on how to use these materials. McVeigh and Kenny discussed where they could purchase military grade explosives. Kenny agreed to research this through his associates. On December 7, McVeigh met with other ARA members in Ohio before traveling back to Kansas.

The Midwest Bank Bandits robbed a bank in a Cleveland suburb on December 8, and the gang returned to Kansas. McVeigh was present at a gun show in Overland Park, where he was selling bumper stickers, books and flags. Also present at that gun show were ARA members Langan, Scott Stedeford and Kevin McCarthy.

Between December 13 and 16, McVeigh traveled from Kansas to Arizona, where he stored some bomb-making parts. He and Mike Fortier then traveled back to Kansas. They stopped for an overnight stay at a Motel 6 in Amarillo, Texas. On December 16, they traveled through Oklahoma City, where McVeigh told me he pointed out the Murrah Building to Fortier and identified it as his target for the bombing.

During his days in Arizona, McVeigh carefully cultivated his relationship with numerous right-wing Patriot types. Those included Richard Kaufman, head of the Arizona chapter of National Alliance in Mohave Valley. The founder of that organization was Dr. William Pierce, author of *The Turner Diaries*. McVeigh's association with Kaufman is well documented in telephone records, FBI interview statements and by eyewitnesses. Johnny Bangerter, a leader of the Army of Israel, a skinhead group in the Arizona and Utah area, told FBI agents that Kaufman introduced him to McVeigh in early 1995.

McVeigh was a busy man during this period, as he coordinated the planning and strategic aspects of the Oklahoma City Bombing, now just a few months away. Dealing with the criminal element and those on the fringes of the Aryan movement, with their own egos and agendas, was a daunting task for former United States Army Sgt. McVeigh. He told me: "Our mission required skill, timing and adherence to a stringent schedule. These guys were, for the most part, lifetime fuckups, not trained and disciplined soldiers ready for action anytime or anywhere."

Some perspective on McVeigh's recruiting efforts during this period comes from Bangerter. He told the FBI he met McVeigh during the Crossroads of the West gun show in St. George, Utah, on February 25-27, 1995. Mike Fortier testified that he and McVeigh were staying at the Dixie Palms Motel in St. George on those dates, and Fortier's statements to the FBI confirm that he had obtained contact information for Bangerter's skinhead group at McVeigh's behest. Bangerter told the FBI that McVeigh met with various Aryan and white supremacist members while he was in Utah.

According to McVeigh, Fortier had already backed out of participating in the bombing, and Shawn Kenny had joined the Army earlier that month. McVeigh told me he was disappointed that two of his recruits had "flaked out." He was having difficulties finding men he could trust. "They seemed to be a lot of talkers," he said. Interestingly, in a defense memo dated January 11, 1996, one of McVeigh's defense team members, Robert Warren, wrote: "I feel it is important to note a comment that Tim has made on more than one occasion, 'those who do the most talking usually take the least action.' It is clear that Tim was a talker to the highest extreme. . . Is he (McVeigh) both a talker and an actor?"

McVeigh expanded on this subject during our conversations. He had high praise for many he had recruited, but was scornful of Fortier, saying: "Look at Mike. I gave him weapons valued at ten to twenty thousand dollars, schooled him on how to sell the merchandise at gun shows and he still couldn't do it effectively. He was in the Army and didn't learn shit. His only claim to fame is being a speed freak and rattin' on me."

McVeigh's evaluation of the ARA members was very different: "Those guys, even Langan, were well disciplined. Ask yourself this: How did they get that way? Fuckin' practice – we drilled and we practiced. Just like we practiced in the desert before the bombing."

It is a known fact that McVeigh and the ARA were in the Arizona desert in February and March 1995. He told me that he and ARA members Peter Langan, (nicknamed "Commander Pedro"), Richard Guthrie and Kevin McCarthy met several times for "dry runs" of "planting the bomb and getting away." Guthrie, who was ex-Navy, was in charge of the ARA for McVeigh's use of the team. McVeigh said: "I just felt uneasy about Commander Pedro. What kind of a handle is that? I never suspected him of being a fag or a rat, though."

McVeigh was having real trouble finding last-minute replacements for the recruits who had backed out of the bombing. It's possible this was because some in the Aryan, neo-Nazi and skinhead community suspected McVeigh was a federal agent. According to the March 9, 1996, memo by McVeigh's investigator Richard Reyna, he interviewed a man named Jim Dalton. Dalton stated that in early February 1995, he was in the office of a newsmagazine in LaVerkin, Utah, (the same town where Johnny Bangerter resided), when he received a telephone call from someone calling himself "Chuck." The man told Dalton he wanted to build a motel in St. George, but he did not want to use any "niggers" or "spics," that he just wanted to use white supremacists, and that they could meet at the Dixie Palms Motel in St. George, where he was staying. (Dalton later identified "Chuck" as Timothy McVeigh, based on his motel registration at the Dixie Palms.)

Dalton claimed he did get the word out to various people, including several skinheads, but they suspected the caller was a federal agent, and not a very convincing one. No one attended the meeting.

Dalton told Reyna he believed Timothy McVeigh was a federal agent or someone under the control of the federal government, who was attempting to infiltrate the skinhead movement. Dalton claims to have obtained that information through his contacts within the CIA and other federal agencies.

During February and March 1995, McVeigh threaded his way through Arizona, Nevada, Utah, Colorado, Kansas, Missouri, Illinois, Michigan and Oklahoma. Most of these trips were brief and all were by way of driving. Much has been made of McVeigh's use of old vehicles and their shabby conditions. According to McVeigh, using an alias, he purchased a four-wheel drive SUV that he kept parked away from his "home base of operations." He told me: "I used that SUV for long-distance travel and took cabs after parking it. The rundown vehicles were all a part of the facade." He laughed at how easy it had been to fool "the public and later on, my lawyers." McVeigh may have fooled his lawyers, but certainly not his investigator. In a report dated December 12, 1995, Reyna stated that after a discussion with McVeigh relating to Roger Moore, Terry Nichols and the subject of explosives, "I looked at Mr. McVeigh and smiled then told him that he was full of shit!" Most of McVeigh's legal team found it impossible to believe much of the story he told them about his planning and preparation for the bombing. His records are replete with notations documenting their suspicions and his failure to pass polygraph examinations administered at the request of his legal team.

McVeigh's travels and actions have been difficult for those in law enforcement and others to track. He is known to have used at least 10 alias names, which include Daryl Bridges, David Gilmore, Mike Havens, Tim Johnson, Bob Kling, Shawn Masters, Richard Menton, Steve Murphy, Shawn Rivers and Tim Tuttle. He told me he had used so many aliases that he couldn't even remember them all.

It was now two months before the bombing. At a second meeting in Las Vegas between McVeigh and the Major, on March 17, 1995, the Major introduced McVeigh to a man he referred to as "Poindexter." According to McVeigh, Poindexter was the Major's choice for building the bombs – plural: there would be more than one. The Major now instructed McVeigh to check in every day until the mission was completed.

While in Las Vegas, McVeigh also met with Cheyne Kehoe in order to collect money that was owed McVeigh from the sale of meth. Kehoe paid McVeigh $8,000, and they parted ways. He had just taken possession of $7,900 in counterfeit currency.

McVeigh traveled to Colorado for another meeting with a contact at Executive Security International, who provided some instructions in the area of explosives. While in Colorado at a gas station, an angry manager confronted McVeigh as he paid for "gas and some munchies." The man informed McVeigh that his two $20 bills were fake, McVeigh stated: "It seems that the ink had rubbed off." McVeigh was as surprised as the manager, and immediately paid with a good $100 bill and drove away "like a bat outta hell." Avoiding scrutiny by law enforcement, even a "local cop or a county Mountie was my goal," McVeigh said. When recounting this event, he speculated on how such a screw-up could have been disastrous for "the mission."

During a check-in call to the Major in March, McVeigh reported on a recent meeting that he had attended with Andreas Strassmeir and his associate Michael Brescia in Elohim City. During that meeting McVeigh learned that the State of Arkansas had set April 19 as the date on which it would execute CSA member Richard Snell. Those at Elohim City and many others in anti-government circles around the country saw the selection of that date as a slap in the face, and as intentional disrespect and dishonor to all of the Waco victims. McVeigh felt there was a certain amount of irony in that event coinciding with his own mission. However, he was strictly focused on the importance of his mission. An execution just couldn't compare.

During that same call to the Major, McVeigh reported his selection of Brescia as the person who would assist him in delivering the truck bomb to the target. At Strassmeir's urging, Brescia had readily agreed.

In a letter to his sister Jennifer dated March 25, 1995, McVeigh stated that something big was going to happen in the month of the bull. According to her FBI interview statement, Jennifer took this to mean March or April. That letter instructed Jennifer not to send any mail to McVeigh after April 1, as he might not get it in time, or: "G-men might get it out of my box, incriminating you." McVeigh also referenced his sister as being a rock, who would be able to withstand questioning. He advised his sister that she might want to stay away from home by extending her vacation.

In my conversations with McVeigh, he often spoke of Jennifer and how he trusted her unconditionally. He said she understood why he was carrying out his mission. He showed genuine emotion and concern when speaking about his little sister. The only time I ever saw any anger from McVeigh directed at her was after some media outlets broadcast reports of her working as a stripper and jello-wrestling in a club. McVeigh was angry with the media for reporting she had changed her name, and angry with her for taking up such activities. I quizzed McVeigh about her testimony against him. He said: "I expected her to do what she had to do. Nothing she could say or do could hurt me. I put her in that situation with full knowledge of the consequences."

On March 31, 1995, McVeigh rented a room at the Imperial Motel on Route 66 in Kingman. He gave his address as Fort Riley, Kansas. He told me he intentionally used his own name and identification to leave a paper trail. He said he wanted "a blind man to be able to see that trail." According to McVeigh, he wasn't alone at the Imperial Motel, but had a steady stream of visitors, including associates in the Arizona Patriots militia. McVeigh and Poindexter inventoried the ingredients on hand for making the bomb.

April 1995: The bombing was now just days away. McVeigh and Poindexter spent the first week of the month in Kingman. McVeigh told me he was surprised that no one in the media ever picked up on the fact that he regularly registered in motels as a single occupant even when others were with him. He did so in order to get a lower rate, and referred to this practice as being "thrifty."

Using the alias Daryl Bridges, McVeigh had obtained a telephone calling card from The Spotlight newspaper as part of his cover. Records from that phone account show that between April 5 and 7, McVeigh made nine brief telephone calls from the Imperial Motel to the Arizona chapter of National Alliance. When explaining to me his contacts with members of this organization, McVeigh insisted he knew the feds would backtrack his every move, and it was important that they find the right-wing connections. "I left a map of movements and transactions exactly as instructed," he said.

It is widely known that McVeigh placed a call to Andreas Strassmeir at Elohim City on April 5. According to Rev. Millar's daughter-in-law

Joan, who answered the phone, the caller asked to speak to "Andy." When advised that Strassmeir wasn't available, McVeigh told me he left a message saying: "Tell Andy I'll be coming through." This call is also traced to the Daryl Bridges calling card.

During the two weeks leading up to the bombing, McVeigh told me that he was in regular contact with the Major and with Roger Moore. McVeigh said Moore was helpful with arranging last-minute contacts.

On April 7, McVeigh left Kingman and drove to Tulsa, where he met with Strassmeir and Brescia. That meeting took place the following day and evening. McVeigh told me they discussed the plan to bomb the Murrah Building, and that he gave Strassmeir $12,000 to be used in a "decoy operation," in which a box-type truck without explosives would be driven to Oklahoma City. McVeigh said the purpose of this decoy truck was to confuse and frustrate investigators after the bombing. McVeigh wanted the decoy truck painted yellow to resemble a Ryder truck. But the truck Strassmeir delivered didn't satisfy McVeigh. He recalled: "It was an ugly mustard yellow, and I wanted it to be as identical to a Ryder truck as possible. A detail such as color is important."

Reporter J.D. Cash has verified McVeigh's claims that he met with Strassmeir and Brescia on April 8. Cash was the first reporter to discover the existence of at least five dancers at Lady Godiva's strip club in Tulsa, who identified all three men as being in the club on that date. In an interview with a CBS reporter, the dancers stated they were positive that McVeigh and Strassmeir were together in the club just 11 days before the bombing. Additionally, the bouncer at Lady Godiva's claimed to have seen a faded Ryder truck in the parking lot that night.

McVeigh spent most of April 9 in and around Oklahoma City, including a trip to a local flea market. He said: "I wanted to get a feel for the people there. In a matter of days, their lives would never be the same." The Murrah Building was closed that Sunday. McVeigh told me he didn't even drive by the building that day. He met with Richard Guthrie at a local Pancake House restaurant near St. Anthony's Hospital on 10th Street. With Guthrie at the wheel of his tan-colored pickup truck, McVeigh and Guthrie drove around checking the highways and turnpikes leading into and from Oklahoma City. After satisfying themselves there were no ongoing road construction projects requiring detours, according to McVeigh, they returned to his vehicle and drove to Kansas in a two-car caravan.

Kevin McCarthy and Scott Stedeford were waiting in a Ryder truck at Geary State Fishing Park located south of Junction City, Kansas. McVeigh and Guthrie, traveling in Guthrie's pickup truck, arrived for a meeting in the park on April 10. They had made an overnight stop at the ARA safe house in Pittsburg, Kansas, on the way.

Much has been made of a telephone call made from the Imperial Motel in Kingman on April 11. McVeigh told me: "It's very simple. I didn't make the fuckin' call. Poindexter did!" McVeigh told me Poindexter was in Kingman with the explosives and McVeigh's SUV, and that Poindexter then traveled from Arizona to Kansas bringing with him all of the bomb-making materials from a storage locker in Kingman.

Two witnesses verify seeing a Ryder truck, a brown pickup truck and a white car for two days at the fishing park at Geary Lake. These witnesses are James Sargent and Georgia Rucker. A third witness, Army Sgt. Tom Herington, reported seeing a Ryder truck at the same location on April 10 -12. All three witnesses agree on these dates. This was several days before McVeigh picked up the Ryder truck he would use to deliver the bomb.

According to McVeigh, several members of the ARA camped at Geary State Park for a few days using the decoy truck as a camper for sleeping. This was all a part of the decoy operation. The truck was purposely parked there in plain sight. McVeigh told me that Michael Brescia drove the newly painted decoy truck from Tulsa to Junction City.

McVeigh provided conflicting accounts of his whereabouts on Wednesday and Thursday, April 12 and 13. As with much of what he told me, the truth most likely lies somewhere in the middle. If, as McVeigh told me on some occasions, he was at Geary Lake on April 10, meeting with the ARA gang, then the surveillance camera video taken by the FBI from the Terrible Herbst convenience store in Kingman, Arizona, on April 11, which depicts a white male resembling McVeigh, must be someone else. The man is seen in the store alone. He leaves, then returns 11 minutes later. No official source has ever positively identified this person as McVeigh. However, the video was used as a part of the government's timeline for McVeigh's movements prior to the bombing.

It is possible that McVeigh was, in fact, in Arizona on April 11. On some occasions, he told his legal team that he checked out of his motel in Kingman on Wednesday, April 12. Witnesses place McVeigh at the Murrah Building in Oklahoma City the next day, Thursday, April 13. McVeigh has claimed that he and Michael Fortier were both at the Murrah Building that day, but that neither man went inside. This claim seems to defy logic, however, if McVeigh's statement regarding Fortier's unwillingness to assist him with the bombing was true.

When I confronted McVeigh about Fortier's involvement in the bombing, McVeigh refused to provide straight answers. He only did so when he was angered by something Michael or Lori Fortier did or said that was reported by the media. At those times McVeigh would say of Fortier: "He should be in a cell right here with me." However, most of the time McVeigh appeared to have a certain loyalty toward Fortier. I specifically asked McVeigh: "Tim, how can you take up for the dude? He testified against you and helped the government convict you?" McVeigh replied with a wily grin: "There's more to that story than meets the eye." I pressed harder on this point, reminding McVeigh of our agreement that he would provide truthful, verifiable information. His response was immediate: "Hammer, therein lies the problem. This is something that can never be verified, and the truth is, what difference does it make?"

According to Fortier's many FBI interview statements, he has no specific recollection of what he did during the time period from Monday, April 17, through Wednesday, April 19, other than being around his house in Kingman. He stated that two other people observed him and knew of his whereabouts for that time period. They are his wife Lori and his neighbor James Rosencrans, the known drug dealer and FBI informant. Fortier claims he first heard that the Murrah Building had been blown up while watching *CNN* at a neighbor's house.

By Friday, April 14, McVeigh's path becomes easier to follow. On that day, in Junction City, Kansas, he purchased a 1977 model Mercury Marquis for $250 from a Firestone tire outlet. Richard Guthrie, known for his skills as a shade-tree mechanic, tinkered with the car and assured McVeigh that it was up to the task of transporting him away from Oklahoma City if need be. McVeigh told me the old Mercury was a backup getaway vehicle, to be used only in an emergency if something went wrong.

Later that day, McVeigh checked into the Dreamland Motel in Junction City. This older motel just off Interstate 70 was perfect for his needs. He registered under his own name. He received permission to park a truck in the parking lot. McVeigh claimed to have pulled his "thrifty routine" at the Dreamland because he was not staying alone in the room. When I pressed McVeigh as to why he would take a chance of attracting attention over something so trivial, he just shrugged his shoulders and smiled, saying "there was a method to my madness."

On Saturday, April 15, McVeigh, Terry Nichols and Richard Guthrie met to plan retrieving the bomb-making materials from a storage facility. It was decided that Brescia and Guthrie, with Nichols' help, would load the materials into the pickup truck and then transport them for off-loading onto one of two Ryder trucks that were to be used by the bombers. McVeigh himself had already paid for the rental of one Ryder truck, using the name Robert Kling. He would take possession of that truck on Monday, April 17.

McVeigh told me he rented the second Ryder truck, using the alias Timothy Tuttle, from a Ryder rental agency in St. Paul, Minnesota. This claim has support in FBI files, and in McVeigh's defense team's files. In a memo dated January 7, 1997, issued to Stephen Jones and Rob Nigh under the subject heading "Other Ryder Trucks and Another Grand Jury," the author, Amber McLaughlin, details an FBI interview statement: "According to the attached FBI 302 #1803, there was a grand jury in Minneapolis, Minnesota, investigating the bombing of the Alfred P. Murrah Building in Late April and May, 1995. On April 26, 1995, they subpoenaed phone records from the Ryder Truck Rental in North St. Paul, Minnesota."

There is little doubt that more than one Ryder truck was used in the Oklahoma City Bombing. Interview statements from various people have detailed their accounts of multiple Ryder trucks observed in Kansas and Oklahoma City in the days leading up to the bombing and on Wednesday, April 19, 1995.

McVeigh and Guthrie spent the evening of April 15 in Junction City, going over plans for the 200-mile trip to Oklahoma City. They met in a local bar and drank beer. Guthrie reassured McVeigh that the Mercury would be reliable transportation for his limited needs. After several hours they went back to their respective motels. McVeigh stressed to me that everyone in the ARA knew him as Tim Tuttle, not Tim McVeigh. He laughed and proclaimed: "I bet they were surprised to see my perp walk with a strange name attached to the images." This seemed to somehow amuse him.

On Easter Sunday, April 16, McVeigh picked up the decoy truck that the ARA crew had been using as a camper and parked it at the Dreamland Motel. Witnesses saw what they described as a Ryder truck parked there on that day, a full day before McVeigh took possession of the Ryder truck he had rented locally.

Richard Guthrie and the ARA members were enjoying some creature comforts before the next stage of the mission. Roughing it at Geary Lake had left them bored and ready for some relaxation. ARA member Pete Langan had arrived, driving his white Buick, four-door sedan, the exact type of car witnesses said they saw with a Ryder truck at Geary State Park.

Later that Easter Sunday, McVeigh, Guthrie and Brescia drove to Oklahoma City. McVeigh and Brescia were in the Mercury Marquis, with Guthrie following in his pickup truck. The pickup was loaded with blasting caps and detonators in taped-up cardboard boxes. McVeigh told me that in Oklahoma City, the getaway car was parked and wiped down for prints in a hasty way: "We didn't want to attract any attention." Once in Oklahoma City McVeigh said they stored this material in a "drive-in warehouse off of west Reno. We stashed it quickly and left. I then called the Major to report on our progress and to insure that the other aspects needed for the bombing would be in place on time."

The importance of the warehouse cannot be overstated. During a search of McVeigh's Mercury Marquis after he was identified as the bomber, law enforcement found a handwritten note that contained directions to "EMRICK's Storage." Emrick's Allied Storage is located at 4021 N.W. 3rd Street in Oklahoma City. In an FBI interview statement dated June 8, 1995, Special Agent Donna C. Samson reported that most of the military work done by Emrick's was for military personnel working at Tinker Air Force Base. Military storage is long-term storage for government military material and equipment, including vehicles.

This storage warehouse is located just a few blocks off West Reno, just as McVeigh described to me. My investigator has verified that Emrick's Allied Storage was in business in 1995. It is unknown why Special Agent Samson and Oklahoma City Police Detective Charles Provines, who accompanied her in her investigation, were focusing on the military aspect of Emrick's Allied Storage. Could it be because McVeigh's actions were, as he claimed, part of a military unit mission, and that he was acting as a government agent?

McVeigh placed a call from Oklahoma City to Terry Nichols in the afternoon on that Easter Sunday. He told Nichols that he had car problems and needed him to travel to Oklahoma City to pick him up. McVeigh instructed Nichols to tell his wife Marife that he was in Omaha. McVeigh didn't want Nichols' wife knowing he was in Oklahoma City. Josh Nichols, Terry's son, remembers the call and that McVeigh was screaming in the background.

Guthrie and Brescia had left Oklahoma City to meet with Strassmeir and Dennis Mahon in Tulsa. They needed to finalize plans and update Strassmeir on progress made up to that point. After the meeting Guthrie and Brescia drove back to Junction City.

Nichol's April 21-22 FBI interview statement contains his account of picking up McVeigh in Oklahoma City, their return trip, and McVeigh's claims that "you will see something big in the future." Nichols said he dropped McVeigh off at the Dreamland Motel in Junction City before returning to his home in Herington in the early hours of Monday, April 17.

Back at the Dreamland Motel, McVeigh went to his room, which he was then sharing with Michael Brescia. He had returned from Oklahoma City with Guthrie only an hour or so before. The men slept, showered, and were up and ready for what McVeigh called the "final 48-hour countdown."

That afternoon, McVeigh and Brescia met at a local McDonalds. They drove to Elliot's Body Shop. McVeigh had already paid the rental on the Ryder truck for a four-day trip to Omaha, Nebraska. The dates for the rental ran from April 17-21. McVeigh and Brescia entered the establishment and, after a brief exchange, some paperwork and conversation, they left, Brescia driving Langan's white Buick and McVeigh in the Ryder truck.

I questioned McVeigh at length about whom he was with when he took possession of the Ryder truck. His story never wavered. He insisted he was with Brescia, but that Richard Guthrie had been in the body shop shortly before they arrived. Guthrie had cased the scene for any signs of law enforcement. McVeigh explained: "We were taking extra precautions at each step of the mission."

Several witnesses said they saw a Ryder truck at Geary Lake between April 10 and April 17, prior to McVeigh taking possession of the actual bomb truck that Monday afternoon. Up to five men and several vehicles were observed around the Ryder truck during that time.

McVeigh said he spent Monday night, April 17, alone at the Dreamland Motel, and left his room there for the final time at around 4:30 a.m. on Tuesday, April 18. He drove to a nearby motel where Brescia was waiting. They then drove together to the storage locker in Herington. As planned, Poindexter was there when they arrived in the Ryder truck. Working together, they loaded the truck with empty barrels and drums filled with liquid nitromethane. Using a hand dolly, they were able to move the heavy drums, which weighed approximately 350 to 400 pounds each, up the ramp and into the cargo area. They also loaded crates of other explosives, including tovex and Kinestik, into the SUV that was driven by Poindexter. Other items, including buckets and 55-gallon plastic drums, also went into the truck.

I questioned McVeigh repeatedly about who was at the storage facility that morning. McVeigh said Nichols was a no-show that morning. McVeigh said "Wild Bill" Guthrie and McCarthy provided perimeter security: "They were armed, as we all were, but Wild Bill wasn't going to let some Johnny Q. Citizen walk up on us. He sure as hell wasn't going to let some security guard or cop drive up." McVeigh made wild hand gestures and paced the recreation cage

Deadly Secrets 71

as he told me this. It was as if he was reliving that early morning prior to the bombing. It was obvious he was still caught up in the moment.

If true, McVeigh's account of the bomb-building operation would significantly alter the story of the crime – and especially the role of Terry Nichols, since, according to the government's case against them, McVeigh and Nichols were supposed to have built the bomb by themselves at Geary Lake on Tuesday, April 18.

At one point McVeigh told me that he and Nichols constructed a "half-ass bomb," but that it was not the bomb he used to blow up the Murrah Building. This account is consistent with a sworn declaration dated February 9, 2007, in which Nichols describes in detail the bomb that he and McVeigh constructed. The timeframe is inconsistent, however. McVeigh was obviously not at both Geary Lake and the Herington storage locker on the morning of April 18. Nichols' declaration was filed in court as part of a lawsuit brought by Jesse Trentadue against the FBI under the Freedom of Information Act.

Nichols stated:

> On the morning of April 18, 1995, I was at Geary Lake and helped McVeigh construct a bomb. The bomb that I helped McVeigh build that morning did not resemble in any fashion the bomb McVeigh described in *American Terrorist*. The Bomb was constructed and comprised of the metal and white plastic barrels (six each, they were black metal and white plastic) which I mentioned previously. There were no blue plastic barrels. The bomb was a V shape, not a backwards J shape and it took up only about half of the truck, not almost the entire truck as McVeigh's design would require as described in *American Terrorist*.
>
> The Ammonium nitrate fertilizer used in the bomb was a problem. It had been exposed to water and moisture as a result of being stored since its purchase in the fall of 1994. Consequently, much of the fertilizer had solidified so that it was lumpy. McVeigh broke the bags of solidified fertilizer into smaller chunks

and dropped them into the barrels. This worked well for the metal barrels with removable tops, but the lumpy fertilizer was a problem for the white plastic barrels, which could only be accessed by a small 3 inch bunghole. McVeigh shoved smaller solidified chunks of ammonium nitrate fertilizer into these plastic barrels through the bungholes.

Altogether, between 90 and 92 fifty pound bags of fertilizer were used and 80 went into the barrels. To the rear of the V by the barrels, we stacked the remaining 10 to 12 bags of ammonium nitrate fertilizer that had been soaked in fuel oil since there was not enough nitromethane. The treated wooden poles were nailed to the floor of the truck to keep the barrels from shifting. As I mentioned earlier, I do not know what McVeigh did with the 7-1/2 cases of Tovex taken from the Marion Quarry and not used in the construction of the bomb at Geary Lake on the morning of April 18, 1995, but McVeigh was planning another bombing later.

Although the timeframe does not match, Nichols' sworn statement is consistent with McVeigh's claims that he made more than one bomb and that two Ryder trucks and a decoy truck were used in the mission. Other physical evidence and FBI interview statements substantiate those claims as well.

At 8:00 a.m. on Tuesday, April 18, McVeigh, Brescia and Poindexter, in a two-vehicle convoy, met Guthrie and Langan at a McDonald's just off I-70. Guthrie was driving the second Ryder truck, with the Nichols/McVeigh-constructed bomb inside. Langan drove Guthrie's pickup. McCarthy and Scott Stedeford arrived a short time later driving Langan's Buick. Brescia then left with Langan to retrieve the decoy truck that carried a cargo of weapons, police scanners and communication equipment. The two Ryder trucks driven by McVeigh and Guthrie, followed by Poindexter in the SUV, left Junction City for Oklahoma City.

Because the events and actions of April 18-19 are most critical, and because as far as the world knows, it was just McVeigh who set off the deadly bomb, I quizzed Timothy McVeigh many times as to who did what and when the day before and the day of the Oklahoma City Bombing. I took notes and would pose suggestive questions to see if McVeigh would change his story. For that reason, I am able to write with confidence that the facts as detailed here are exactly as McVeigh told them to me. He never changed any of the facts as they relate to the ARA members.

It should be noted here that Peter Langan has stated many times that he has information about the Oklahoma City Bombing: specifically, that he knows that some of his fellow ARA gang members were McVeigh accomplices in the bombing. Langan has attempted unsuccessfully to parlay this information into a deal to win his freedom from prison. But Langan also says he never personally met Timothy McVeigh, that he was not present in Oklahoma City or personally involved in the Oklahoma City Bombing in any way. Langan has never stated he didn't meet and know Tim Tuttle.

From a truck plaza en route to Oklahoma City, McVeigh alerted the Major of their estimated arrival time. McVeigh agreed to meet the Major and his team at the warehouse where the bomb would be assembled. The meeting was set for 11:00 p.m. Tuesday night, April 18. The finalized plans would be discussed and the Major could inspect the finished bomb.

After arriving in Oklahoma City, all three vehicles drove to a truck stop off I-40 where one of the Ryder trucks was parked with the already assembled bomb inside. With Guthrie driving McVeigh's Ryder truck, and with Poindexter and McVeigh trailing, they traveled to the storage warehouse.

During the following hours, Poindexter, with the help of McVeigh and Guthrie, built a 7000-pound bomb out of the assembled ingredients. In addition to the homemade elements of the bomb, military grade explosives were added to the mixture of ammonium nitrate and fuel oil, known as ANFO. These added explosives were intended to make the bomb more powerful without being easily detectable by investigators. McVeigh told me: "This stuff worried me. It was the only part of the bomb which couldn't have been easily homegrown," meaning ingredients that were not available on the open market. Poindexter assured McVeigh that this was what the Major had instructed him to do. By 9:30 p.m. on April 18, the bomb was completed and the three men left the warehouse for something to eat.

Before returning to the warehouse for his meeting with the Major, McVeigh dropped Guthrie off at a motel in the area of I-40 and MacArthur. Guthrie, McVeigh and Brescia had a brief conversation. McVeigh and Poindexter traveled back to the warehouse while Guthrie and Brescia retrieved the McVeigh/Nichols bomb truck from the truck stop. Brescia and other ARA members had rented rooms at the Sands Motel on South Rockwell in Oklahoma City. Guthrie parked one truck in the motel parking lot overnight.

The Major, with his associate Roberto, whom McVeigh had met two years before in New Jersey, arrived at the warehouse. Handshakes all around and then an inspection of the bomb. As McVeigh and the Major talked, Roberto walked up behind Poindexter, who stood admiring his work, and, in one swift motion, "cut his throat from ear to ear," McVeigh recalled. "I jumped, but the Major placed his hand on my shoulder and said, 'Soldier, he was only hired help, not one of us.'" McVeigh and Roberto loaded the body into the Ryder truck with the bomb. McVeigh placed a padlock on the door of the truck's cargo bay and they all left the warehouse. McVeigh explained that he had been surprised by Roberto's actions, but that he understood, because in a mission like this anyone was expendable, himself included.

During McVeigh's conversations with the Major in the warehouse, the Major said that nothing was being left to chance. McVeigh learned that other members of the elite unit had installed C-4 explosives inside the Murrah Federal Building in order to insure maximum damage from the explosion. These devices, as well as the truck bomb, were not rigged with manual fuses as has been widely speculated upon. In fact, McVeigh had been provided a hand-held transmitter that was to be used in detonating the explosives.

At approximately 6:00 a.m. on Wednesday morning, April 19, McVeigh, Brescia and Guthrie traveled from the Sands Motel to the warehouse. They were dropped off by Pete Langan, who returned to the motel to assemble the rest of the ARA crew. They would provide security for the bombing operation. Guthrie, McVeigh and Brescia equipped themselves with headsets and mouthpieces in order to allow for constant radio contact.

By 8:00 a.m. the group left the warehouse. McVeigh was driving the Ryder truck with Poindexter's body and the bomb inside. He was accompanied by both Richard Guthrie and Michael Brescia in the passenger seats of the truck. The ARA team, driving the tan pickup truck and white Buick, were already in place at locations near the Murrah Federal Building in downtown Oklahoma City. Brescia exited the truck at a stoplight about a half block away from the Murrah Building and trailed the truck on foot. As McVeigh pulled up in front of the building, Guthrie exited the truck and directed McVeigh as he pulled into the handicapped-parking zone. Brescia, who had caught up on foot, now stood outside the truck with Guthrie. The time was a few minutes before 9:00 a.m. After McVeigh parked the truck, all three men briskly walked away and McVeigh detonated the bomb.

For whatever reason – and McVeigh never shed any light on this key question in our conversations – Guthrie and Brescia did not pick McVeigh up in his SUV after the bombing, as they were supposed to do. McVeigh went to Plan B, making his way to the Mercury getaway car. Within 10 minutes of the blast, Timothy McVeigh was headed out of Oklahoma City, leaving in his wake utter devastation, destruction, and massive loss of life that at the time constituted the worst act of terrorism ever to occur on American soil. The blast and its aftermath killed 168 men, women and children and seriously injured at least 509 others. In his mind, McVeigh's mission was a success. Not perfect, but then most missions are not.

Approximately 90 minutes after the explosion in Oklahoma City, McVeigh was pulled over as he drove the Mercury getaway car on I-35 towards Kansas. From all appearances, it was a routine traffic stop. Oklahoma State Highway Patrol Trooper Charles S. Hanger stopped McVeigh for not having a license plate on the Mercury. McVeigh, who was armed with a .45 caliber Glock in a shoulder holster and a knife in his belt, exited the yellow Mercury and walked towards the trooper's patrol car. They met about halfway between the vehicles. During a brief exchange, Trooper Hanger noticed the bulge under McVeigh's windbreaker jacket. In short order, and while McVeigh offered no resistance at all, Hanger took him into custody, placed him in handcuffs, searched the Mercury, and confiscated McVeigh's weapon. The Oklahoma City Bomber's fate was sealed.

In hindsight, several puzzling questions stand out about McVeigh's arrest. With news of the bombing streaming over the airwaves, McVeigh's behavior and appearance would seem to have drawn intense suspicion. Not only was he armed and headed for the state border just 90 minutes after the bombing. He was wearing a T-shirt bearing a picture of Abraham Lincoln on the front, with presidential assassin John Wilkes Booth's words, "sic, semper, tyrannis" printed on it. The back of the T-shirt featured a picture of a tree with red blood droplets, along with this Thomas Jefferson quotation: "The tree of liberty must be refreshed from time to time with the blood of patriots and tyrants." Somehow, though, the trooper did not seem to connect the dots that this prisoner might be the Oklahoma City Bomber.

Another puzzling question about the arrest concerns a second vehicle reportedly traveling with McVeigh and pulled over along the highway at the time of his arrest. According to a page-one news story in the *Houston Chronicle* on May 12, 1995, federal authorities were telling reporters that an automatic camera mounted in Trooper Hanger's car taped the McVeigh arrest. The unnamed federal authorities said the trooper's camera captured a brown pickup truck, pulled over in the background, and that the truck belonged to McVeigh's Arizona chemist friend Steven Colbern.

The story, by Dan Thomasson and Peter Copeland of the Scripps Howard News Service, quoted an unidentified federal investigator saying: "The trooper had a hell of a day." According to the news story: "Sophisticated enhancement techniques were used to improve the video until investigators could read the license plate number. The truck, registered to Colbern, contained traces of ammonium nitrate, believed to be the main explosive ingredient used in the bombing."

The very same day this story appeared, Friday, May 12, Steven Colbern, then a federal fugitive wanted on firearms charges unrelated to the bombing, was arrested in Arizona. But by the time of his arraignment on May 13, official speculation that Colbern might be connected to the bombing had suddenly ended. Arizona U.S. Attorney Janet Napolitano personally appeared at the Colbern arraignment and refused to answer questions about whether the FBI was investigating a link between Colbern and the Oklahoma City bombing.

No more information ever surfaced about the brown pickup truck reportedly caught on the McVeigh arrest videotape. In December 2008, when the government released the arrest videotape to the Oklahoma City National Memorial, there were no images of the brown pickup truck on the tape, only images of Trooper Hanger searching the yellow Mercury Marquis after the actual arrest of Timothy McVeigh.

Shortly after 11:00 a.m. on the morning of the bombing, McVeigh was booked into the Noble County Jail in Perry, Oklahoma. He was charged with four misdemeanors that included transporting a loaded firearm in a motor vehicle, unlawfully carrying a weapon, failure to display a current license plate and failing to maintain proof of insurance.

He went through the booking process, attempting to be jovial and friendly with those in the Noble County Sheriff's Department. His actions and demeanor were somewhat out of place, however, considering that a television was broadcasting reports and videotape on the bombing from nearby Oklahoma City. McVeigh was fingerprinted, photographed, dressed in orange jailhouse garb, and placed in a cell.

During the booking procedure, Trooper Hanger made an inventory of the evidence he had taken from McVeigh. The April 19, 1995 records of that procedure do not reflect the badge that Hanger took from McVeigh as a part of the arrest. But an FBI interview statement does. The FBI report states that Trooper Hanger turned in a security badge McVeigh had in his possession several days later, after federal authorities had identified McVeigh as the suspect in the Oklahoma City Bombing.

This badge is certainly interesting, especially in light of Trooper Hanger's apparent delay in turning it in. McVeigh stressed to me repeatedly that the "FBI or ATF switched those badges. I didn't have a fake-ass security badge that wouldn't fool anyone. I had the official badge given to me by the Major."

McVeigh went on to say: "I was never trying to escape capture. My arrest was all a part of the mission. The bombing had to land squarely at the feet of someone involved in the anti-government movement. I left a paper trail that even a blind man could follow. I even left a business card on the seat of the patrol car with a handwritten note about dynamite on it."

Witnesses at the Noble County Jail claimed that McVeigh made several telephone calls during his stay there. At least one of those calls was reportedly to his friend and comrade Roger Moore. According to Diana Sanders Burke, a former bail bond agent in Wagoner, Oklahoma, Burke had posted bond for Roger Moore in November 1993. She said she had firsthand knowledge that, two years later, Moore attempted to arrange bond for McVeigh while he was confined on the misdemeanor charges in Perry, Oklahoma. Burke told an investigator for Terry Nichols that Moore called a bondsman for the Charles Smith agency to ask about posting bond for McVeigh. According to Burke, Moore told the bondsman McVeigh was not a bad guy and that the feds were just trying to set him up.

Telephone records reveal that calls were also made from the Noble County Jail on Thursday, April 20, at 6:37 p.m. and Friday, April 21, 1995, at 11:15 a.m. to bail bondsman Roger Brett Goad, doing business as Coldrion Candy Bail Bonds in Pawnee, Oklahoma. Goad reported that he accepted one collect telephone call from McVeigh on April 20, 1995. McVeigh mentioned that his father and a friend could help in posting bond. Clearly, McVeigh wanted out of jail. Goad informed McVeigh to call back once a judge had set the amount of his bail. Goad said he never heard back from McVeigh.

The next day, Friday, April 21, the FBI closed in, naming McVeigh as the Oklahoma City Bomber and parading him before television cameras in a perp walk designed to send the message that the FBI had its man.

Still, mysteries lingered about McVeigh's capture. I questioned him about the missing license plate from the getaway car, that puzzling little detail that led to his arrest after such a carefully laid plan. But McVeigh gave conflicting responses. At times he would claim the missing plate was all a part of "the plan." At other times, he would be visibly angry and state that someone had betrayed him, that the license plate had been removed without his knowledge, or that it "just fell off." When I suggested a missing license plate was certainly a way to attract the attention of the police, and especially following an event such as the bombing, he looked at me with unbridled hatred in his eyes and said: "Hammer, do you think I'm stupid? Don't you fuckin' think that I'd have better sense than to remove that tag?"

When I suggested that maybe someone wanted him to get arrested, he replied: "Of course they did, but it wasn't supposed to happen when and how it did." I suggested to him that perhaps he had only been a pawn or a patsy to be left holding the bag for others. He became furious and exclaimed: "I'm nobody's goddamn patsy."

McVeigh then went into the official lone-wolf version of how he, and he alone, had masterminded the bombing, that he was always in control, and that the decisions were his. When reminded of facts to the contrary that he had already provided, which had been verified, McVeigh hollered for a guard and asked to be taken back to his cell.

No one has ever cleared up this mystery, but years later, Terry Nichols added his own recollection. In his 2007 sworn declaration, Nichols recounts: "On Thursday, April 20, 1995, I went to the Herington, Kansas storage shed where McVeigh kept some of his things. In that shed I found the rear license plate from the yellow Mercury McVeigh was driving when he was arrested after the bombing. I also found at least one hand grenade. The license plate and hand grenade I threw into a nearby river on Friday morning the 21st (of April, 1995)." Nichols further states: "To this day, I have never understood why McVeigh removed that license plate, which eventually led to his arrest, brought it back to Kansas and deliberately left it in that storage shed among his personal possessions."

Timothy McVeigh: mastermind or patsy?

My friend, the late J.D. Cash spent many years investigating McVeigh and the Oklahoma City Bombing. Cash was an astute reader of character, and one of the few reporters to actually interview Timothy McVeigh face to face, prior to his trial. This is what he wrote: "On 13 February 1996, I interviewed Mr. McVeigh at El Reno Federal Prison, just outside Oklahoma City. I came away impressed by only one thing: Mr. McVeigh was no leader. I found him to be immature and easily manipulated. His hot buttons were fringe right-wing ideology and fantasies involving women. Push those buttons and Sergeant Mac was your boy. The perfect patsy."

Cash was not the only person to reach this conclusion. In a McVeigh defense team memo dated April 19, 1996, one year after the bombing, Attorney Dick Burr reported on the group's assessment of McVeigh after a daylong meeting. "We then talked about whether Tim could have been the leader in the bombing," Burr wrote. "At the beginning of this part of the discussion, Si expressed his view that the attorneys should consider not pushing Tim any further about whether he is lying to us. The leadership qualities seen in Tim in the military have more to do with knowledge than leadership. Tim knew things extremely well in the military, however, he had a hard time communicating what he knew. He felt awkward at it. He would get upset whenever anyone did things wrong, not by the book, particularly when the offender was an officer. He was not very good at thinking on his feet. The general sense was that Tim was not likely the person who came up with the idea for the bombing, but that he could very well have been the person who took responsibility for carrying it out. His strength is in carrying out orders."

McVeigh's investigator, Richard Reyna, authored a fascinating memo dated December 27, 1995, in which he details an interview he had with McVeigh on December 12 of that year. Reyna advised McVeigh that a reporter had interviewed his first court appointed attorney, John W. Coyle (who was relieved of his duties as defense counsel due to a conflict of interest). Coyle told the reporter that McVeigh said "he was operating within the confines of the United States Government when he did what he did." Coyle also stated that McVeigh told him "that he had been recruited by the government while serving a 4-5 month period in the National Guard."

Reyna, the investigator, went on to elaborate further on Coyle's interview with the reporter. Reyna wrote that Coyle said: "Mr. McVeigh was suppose to blow out a few windows in the federal building but that the truck had been switched possibly without his knowledge." According to Reyna, when he reported this to his client: "Mr. McVeigh immediately became angry and yelled out several curse words directed at Mr. Coyle. I immediately asked Mr. McVeigh if there was any truth to what the reporter had reported and Mr. McVeigh replied that parts of what (the reporter) said were true and that other parts were untrue. Before I could ask another question, McVeigh again became angry, and began to curse in a loud voice. Mr. McVeigh stated that Mr. Coyle had no business telling anyone, anything about their private discussions."

Terry Nichols claims he knew that Timothy McVeigh was working as an undercover agent, because McVeigh told him so. In his sworn declaration, Nichols states: "In December of 1992, Timothy McVeigh told me that while he was serving in the U.S. Army, he had been recruited to carry out undercover missions. McVeigh did not say who recruited him, or specify the nature of his mission, He did say, however, that he was to begin making contacts with a network of people after the first of the year and that he was to take no action in furtherance of this mission until called upon. McVeigh said he would be making his first contact down south."

On August 10, 1995, a federal grand jury in Oklahoma City handed down an 11-count indictment in the bombing of the Alfred P. Murrah Federal Building. That indictment contained eight counts of murder for the deaths of federal law enforcement agents, one count of conspiracy to use a weapon of mass destruction, and one count of destruction by use of explosives. The indictment charged Timothy James McVeigh and Terry Lynn Nichols with all 11 counts. Additionally, Count One of the indictment alleged that McVeigh and Nichols "the defendants herein, did knowingly, intentionally, willfully, and maliciously conspire, combine and agree together and with others unknown to the Grand Jury, to use a weapon of mass destruction."

Five years later, after listening to McVeigh's story, I was left wondering: Were these "others unknown" to the grand jury the men McVeigh named in the account of the bombing he gave me?

According to the FBI, at the time of McVeigh's trial, and beyond, there was no known link between McVeigh and the ARA bank robbery gang – no reason for the FBI to investigate them. But, as the rest of my investigation will reveal, that was not true – and the FBI knew it.

At the very same time federal prosecutors were telling juries that McVeigh and Nichols acted alone, the FBI had compelling evidence as to the identities of others unknown. Conclusive proof was coming: the

FBI was deliberately hiding the results of a major probe into the ARA's suspected role in the Oklahoma City Bombing.

But it would take several more years of digging to uncover the truth.

4

CHAPTER FOUR

OTHERS UNKNOWN

The investigation into the bombing of the Murrah Federal Building began immediately after the blast. It involved hundreds of law enforcement officials from jurisdictions including federal, state, county and city. The FBI was the lead agency, but it received assistance from many others, including first responders and ordinary citizens.

By the time of the federal grand jury's indictment in August 1995, federal authorities were locked into their official version of the bombing. Once McVeigh and Nichols became the main suspects, federal investigators seem to have ignored, downplayed, denied or refused to believe others were involved in the conspiracy or the bombing.

It defies logic that McVeigh acted alone in the bombing, considering his own statements, eyewitness accounts and, yes, the government's own investigative records. Government investigators knew of many ties between McVeigh and various right-wing extremist groups. However, the investigators appear to have limited their efforts and concentrated on McVeigh and his associates who might advance the official theory of the crime. In fact, government prosecutors failed to release all of the relevant information and files relating to other suspects in the bombing to McVeigh's legal team as they had been ordered to do.

Just prior to McVeigh's execution, scheduled for May 16, 2001, it was revealed that thousands of pages of documents, including FBI reports, files and other records, had not been disclosed to McVeigh's attorneys prior to his trial in 1997, or during the appellate process. This blunder was a significant one.

At a nationally televised news conference, then Attorney General John D. Ashcroft announced that the execution of Timothy James McVeigh would be postponed until June 11, allowing McVeigh's lawyers time to sort through the documents in question. Ashcroft and the FBI's director insisted that it was only a blunder that had caused this violation of the court's order to disclose all such documents. They assured the public that it was the FBI's incompetence and not some nefarious plot within the Justice Department to withhold documents. Ashcroft went on to state that the materials in question were of no value to McVeigh's defense team. This claim was hotly contested in a bitter battle launched at the eleventh hour.

Ultimately, Judge Richard Matsch ruled that the government's failure to provide the documents as previously ordered had not adversely affected McVeigh's right to a fair trial because the information contained within the files would not have altered the outcome of the trial. The U.S. Court of Appeals for the Tenth Circuit in Denver upheld that decision. McVeigh then decided not to pursue the matter to the United States Supreme Court. His decision to waive further appeals led to his execution on June 11, 2001.

It is clear that throughout the Oklahoma City Bombing case, government agents refused to seek out other suspects once McVeigh, Nichols and the Fortiers had become their targets. The only real question is why? Based upon my investigation and McVeigh's statements to me, the answer to that question seems obvious.

Certain federal law enforcement agents had advance knowledge of the bombing, through information they were receiving from confidential informants. Yet the federal agents failed to take steps to stop the bombing.

This is a shocking notion at first glance. But the evidence to support it is compelling, and comes from inside the government itself. For more than a decade, attorney Jesse C. Trentadue has pursued a series of federal

Freedom of Information requests and lawsuits against the FBI, to force disclosure of government secrets about the bombing.

Federal law enforcement documents obtained by Trentadue reveal that prior to the bombing, federal agents knew about a plot that was unfolding in Elohim City, similar to the one McVeigh described to me. Before the bombing, federal agents were tracking the very same players McVeigh named to me: including Elohim City's paramilitary arms trainer Andreas Strassmeir, the white supremacist leader Dennis Mahon, and members of the Aryan Republican Army, as well as, very possibly, McVeigh himself.

But when the time came to hold McVeigh and Nichols accountable for their crimes, others appear to have escaped justice. Some may even have been rewarded.

Why?

To find that out, it's necessary to go to Elohim City.

5

CHAPTER FIVE

ELOHIM CITY

Elohim City, which means "City of God," occupies 400 acres of land in a rugged and mountainous area of Adair County, Oklahoma, near the Oklahoma-Arkansas border. If there is one common denominator in Timothy McVeigh's revelations, it might be this reclusive Christian Identity community, devoted to white separatism. The paths of almost all the players in the bomb plot as McVeigh described it crossed here – from McVeigh and Strassmeir, to Mahon and the ARA gang members.

On the very day of the bombing, Rev. Millar, the patriarch of Elohim City, was ministering to a notorious white supremacist on Arkansas' Death row, one Richard Snell. In the 1980s, he had plotted to bomb the Murrah Federal Building himself, and Timothy McVeigh knew of those aspirations. Now, on April 19, 1995, Snell, a convicted murderer, was executed on Arkansas' death row, even though Rev. Millar had petitioned Arkansas' governor to move the execution to a less loaded date than the anniversary of the Waco raid.

Coincidence? Perhaps not.

Rev. Millar presided at Snell's funeral at Elohim City the day after the bombing. It wasn't an act of defiance, but observers did say the spirit of the funeral was a celebration of Snell's life, and also, the birthday of Adolph Hitler. If that was true, it was a rare celebration that day in Oklahoma, as dazed rescuers in Oklahoma City desperately searched for bodies in the rubble of the Murrah Building.

It is true, there was no love lost between Elohim City, with its right-wing ideology, and the federal government. But that very polarity created a close union of sorts. This was the open secret, the other Elohim City: a dysfunctional family of undercover informants reporting to various federal law enforcement agencies about the anti-government activities of residents. In the 1990s, there were thought to be so many informants inside Elohim City, reporting to the FBI, ATF and other federal agencies, that the community became known as Alphabet City.

In the most categorical proof that the federal government must have had prior knowledge of the Oklahoma City Bombing, an undercover informant named Carol Howe was reporting on a bombing conspiracy inside Elohim City to her ATF handler for many months prior to the bombing.

Howe, a strikingly beautiful young woman from a wealthy family, had briefly been involved with Dennis Mahon. Howe had contacted the dial-a-racist hotline maintained by Mahon in Tulsa. She told J.D. Cash: "I kinda had a relationship with him (Mahon) for a while. We talked about relationships once, and he said he wasn't interested in settling down with a woman. All he wanted to do was blow up federal buildings. It was also at that same meeting that he shoved his hand down my dress and I thought, well, something else, but now that I think about it, I think he was feeling for a wire."

Mahon and Andreas Strassmeir were good friends. Mahon had a trailer at Elohim City and visited there often. Mahon was the Oklahoma leader of the White Aryan Resistance. In reports to her handler, ATF Agent Angela Finley-Graham, made during 1994 and 1995, Howe provided information relating to many firearms and conspiracy violations. Howe, also known as "Freya" and "Lady MacBeth," provided over 70 reports to Agent Findley-Graham. Howe also secretly videotaped Mahon, and those videotapes show him discussing weapons and altering them to fully automatic weapons. Additionally, he discussed manufacturing silencers and details on how to build and detonate explosives.

Deadly Secrets

Carol Howe

Howe reported that Strassmeir and Mahon were talking about blowing up federal buildings. They even traveled to Oklahoma City to select potential targets for bombings. Howe, whose confidential informant number was 53270-183 or CI-183, reported all of these activities to the ATF prior to the Oklahoma City Bombing. Agent Findley-Graham filed her first report on Howe's information on August 30, 1994. She captioned the report *White Aryan Resistance*.

Howe later identified Timothy McVeigh, Peter Langan, Michael Brescia, Kevin McCarthy, Scott Stedeford, Mark Thomas and others as having been present at Elohim City in the months leading up to the bombing. According to ATF records, Howe was a paid informant for that agency through at least February 1996.

In January 1995, Rev. Millar called together Strassmeir, Brescia and his other soldiers during a Sunday morning service and instructed them to take whatever action was necessary to protect their community from the U.S. government. The Reverend feared a Waco-like raid on the compound. They flew a Branch Davidian flag at Elohim City. Howe's report on this event is dated January 11, 1995.

Howe also reported that Mahon and Strassmeir had cased the IRS building in Tulsa and the Murrah Federal Building in Oklahoma City in November and December of 1994, and again in February 1995. Mahon has always denied any involvement in the bombing, but he has pointed fingers at others, including Strassmeir. Nevertheless, Mahon told reporters that as a revolutionary he would blow up the Federal Building, but at night when it wasn't occupied.

Two important facts stand out relating to Mahon. He was the only person appearing before the grand jury in Oklahoma City who elected to take the Fifth Amendment, which provides that someone may not be forced to give sworn testimony that would incriminate him. Mahon refused to testify about his knowledge or involvement in the bombing. Mahon also claimed never to have been in downtown Oklahoma City. However, when federal agents seized evidence from one of the ARA's storage lockers they discovered a notebook belonging to Richard Guthrie of the ARA. Inside, Guthrie had written an address less than two blocks from where the Murrah Building had once stood. Beside the address was a notation that Guthrie was to meet Mahon there. In a move that shocked even veteran FBI agents, the Justice Department destroyed that evidence even before some of the ARA members' appeals were exhausted. Such destruction violates FBI procedures. J.D. Cash had filed a Freedom of Information Act request, and then an appeal, for copies of the documents. His appeal was still pending when the Justice Department destroyed the evidence from the bank robbery case.

It was reported in July 1997, that according to investigator Jeff Steinberg, Dennis Mahon himself might have become an ATF informant. Steinberg claims that the ATF had charges on Mahon, but dropped them. "He may have been turned," Steinberg said.

Andreas Strassmeir, Elohim City's paramilitary arms trainer, to whom McVeigh attributed a heavy role in the bomb plot, has been alleged to have been an informant for the ATF, and possibly also the German government.

During a 1997 federal trial, in which the government unsuccessfully prosecuted Carol Howe, a senior FBI agent added one more surprising name to the bulging rolls of Elohim City federal informants: Rev. Millar himself.

Informants, it seems, were everywhere in Elohim City, even – or especially – within the ranks of the bank robbers of the ARA, who were frequent visitors. Most of them, sooner or later, became government informants or protected witnesses. Peter Langan had been a Secret Service informant, who signed on to help capture the fugitive Richard Guthrie, but then double-crossed his federal handlers and teamed up with Guthrie. Shawn Kenny was an FBI informant who eventually turned in Guthrie. Rev. Mark Thomas, Kevin McCarthy and Michael Brescia all became government informants or protected witnesses after the bank robbery gang was busted in 1996.

McVeigh himself, if he was telling the truth in his account to me, was feeding the Major information about the bombing conspiracy while participating in ARA bank robberies.

There may have been another, darker twist to the informant dynamic inside the ARA. These weren't just informants. They were criminals, committing criminal acts, sometimes, apparently, while in their capacity as informants. A closer look into the gang's membership reveals just how deadly a combination this may have been.

6

Chapter Six

The Aryan Republican Army

Peter Langan, cofounder of the ARA with Richard Guthrie, has described its goal: to "overthrow the government . . . and to set free the oppressed people of North America."

Langan was born in 1958. His parents were both U.S. government employees assigned to positions in Vietnam. His father was a CIA operative attached to the International Cooperation Administration as a "safety official." His mother worked at the American Embassy in Saigon. He was a bright, inquisitive, pampered child, the youngest of six children. After returning to the United States, the family lived in Wheaton, Maryland. When Langan's father suffered a massive heart attack and died, Pete was suddenly a boy adrift. He turned to drugs and ran away from home. By age 16 he was involved in his first gunfight.

In Daytona Beach, Florida, Langan robbed a man and stole his van. The police, who caught up with Langan soon thereafter, shot him and blew off the tip of his finger. Langan was tried as an adult and served the next four years in what he called "Gladiator School." According to Langan, he was pushed into the Aryan Brotherhood because of a need to survive. The Aryans offered him protection from black and Hispanic gangs that roamed the prison. He was released in 1978.

Langan spent the next 10 years bouncing from one job and city to another. He was married for a short time, fathered a son and attempted to live the straight life. Being an ex-con made it difficult to find employment that paid a decent wage. Langan sought out his childhood friend Guthrie and partnered up with him.

"Wild Bill" Guthrie had a colorful past. He did a five-year stint in the Navy. He completed his training at Redstone Arsenal in Huntsville, Alabama, and graduated from Indian Head, Maryland's prestigious nuclear training facility. Unfortunately for the hotheaded Guthrie, he washed out of the Navy's SEAL program. His Navy career was soon ended when he painted a swastika on a ship, threatened one of his commanding officers and went AWOL. According to Langan, the Navy had figured out that Wild Bill "was a psycho." After doing some time in the brig, Guthrie received a general discharge from the Navy. The U.S. government had trained him to be an explosives expert and then discharged him with a chip on his shoulder.

Guthrie and Langan had both grown up in the Wheaton, Maryland area just outside of Washington, D.C. By early 1992, they had reunited and embarked upon a life of petty crime together, first swindling department stores out of money on refunded items that they had stolen. They later robbed a Pizza Hut and traveled the country separately. The robbery took place in Lavonia, Georgia.

In early 1992, Langan joined the Ohio chapter of the Aryan Nations. His racist views had been strengthened by his attendance at the Covington Identity Church and by his association with an 18-year-old skinhead named Shawn Kenny. They shared similar beliefs, and Kenny regularly held meetings for Bible study and Aryan Nations teachings at his apartment in Elmwood Place.

Following a May, 1992 arrest for the retail scam, Langan and Guthrie traveled to the Aryan Nation's compound in Hayden Lake, Idaho, where they visited with the Rev. Richard Butler, the group's leader, and others. Langan and Guthrie were not impressed by the rhetoric being espoused. As Langan put it: No one spoke with any sincerity of "direct action against the U.S. government or the Jews who control this country." Those in Hayden Lake were losers in the eyes of Langan.

He and Guthrie had sent funds from their scams to help support direct action by the movement. One positive aspect, at least to Langan's way of thinking, was that his trip to the Aryan Nations compound found him being ordained as a minister of the Christian Identity Church. He felt a personal connection to the Identity ideology.

The first members of the ARA were Langan, Guthrie and Shawn Kenny. Initially their revolution took the form of talking about robberies, bombings, assassinations and creating a new government. The trio had an idea, but the ARA's name and mission was far from being materialized as of October 1992, when the three went their separate ways.

Wild Bill continued his travels, visiting various Christian Identity groups and meeting leaders, listening to and studying their messages, reading books on the Aryan movement from individuals such as Louis Beam, William Pierce and Thom Robb. Guthrie visited with Rev. Mark Thomas, Rev. Millar and other figures in the Identity movement. Guthrie's focus was on taking direct action against the U.S. government. He was hell-bent on getting even with those who had rejected him as a military operative.

During the investigation of the 1992 robbery of the Pizza Hut in Lavonia, Georgia, Franklin County Sheriff Hugh Roach discovered that Guthrie had made numerous statements bragging about his intentions to kill President George H.W. Bush. That information was passed along to the Secret Service. They located and raided a mobile home where Wild Bill had been staying, but didn't find him. In November 1992, the feds caught up with Langan at his home in Cincinnati. They busted him on weapons charges, and soon thereafter he was shipped off to Georgia on the robbery charge.

While awaiting trial in Georgia, where he faced a 20-year sentence, Langan received visitors in August 1993. The Secret Service needed his help. They were seeking his old friend Wild Bill. They claimed that the word in the Aryan Nations movement was that Guthrie might be planning to assassinate President Bush.

Langan readily agreed with the agents that Wild Bill was a psycho and could easily be on a mission to kill the President. After a bit of negotiating, Langan agreed to become a Secret Service informant, to seek out Guthrie and rat him out in exchange for assistance on the charges Langan was facing. The agents met with District Attorney

Lindsay Tise, who was prosecuting Langan in Georgia. The agents were able to obtain the DA's assistance in arranging for Langan's release from jail to assist the Secret Service. He was given a bus ticket, some cash, and sent back to Ohio.

By the early fall of 1993, Langan had ditched his Secret Service contacts and partnered up with Guthrie rather than rat him out. Langan made Wild Bill a full partner in his "army" and bestowed upon him the title of Commander Pavell. Langan became Commander Pedro. They were on a mission. It included the overthrow of the government and extermination or deportation of all non-whites and non-Christians in the United States. They would soon travel to Elohim City for a meeting with others on a similar mission.

During Langan's incarceration, Guthrie had teamed up with Shawn Kenny to rob banks. Guthrie had successfully pulled off two robberies in Cincinnati, and Kenny was involved far more than some realize. He joined Guthrie in the planning and other aspects of the robberies, but was never implicated or investigated by authorities. Kenny did eventually admit, while he was an informant for the government, he helped in planning a third bank robbery.

Wild Bill also became acquainted with other individuals who became full-fledged members of the ARA. They included Mark Thomas, Kevin McCarthy and Scott Stedeford, whom Guthrie had first met in Pennsylvania at Thomas's farm. Thomas was a well-known figure in the Christian Identity movement, and his message was well received by many youths who visited him on a regular basis. In the 1990s, Thomas, a local Aryan Nations leader, hosted numerous skinhead and neo-Nazi rallies such as White Pride Day and the annual Hitler Youth Festival, where participants engaged in activities such as pagan rituals, flag burnings and cross burnings. During one of these events, Thomas introduced Kevin McCarthy, a teenage bass player in the white power band *Day of the Sword*, to Pennsylvania native Scott Stedeford, who himself was an artist and rock musician.

Thomas was also instrumental in introducing McCarthy and Stedeford to a 24-year-old college student from La Salle University named Michael Brescia. He was a Philadelphia native and rock musician. The three new members of the ARA went on to form the speed metal band called *Cyanide*.

Thomas, McCarthy, Stedeford and Brescia traveled separately to Elohim City in the fall of 1994. Thomas and Elohim City's Rev. Millar were old friends. Thomas often encouraged those who attended his gatherings in Pennsylvania to spend time in Elohim City. He actively advised them to undergo the paramilitary training offered there.

In Elohim City, McCarthy, Brescia and Stedeford became roommates with Andreas Strassmeir, who instructed them in all types of weapons training. Strassmeir, also known as Mr. Red, had a vigorous routine he put the recruits through. It included months of target practice, live-fire exercises, swimming through icy water in wintertime, and surviving outdoors without water, food or weapons. In no time Brescia became Strassmeir's second in command. Brescia also became engaged to one of Millar's granddaughters with his blessing. Elohim City was now home to at least three of the ARA's members. All ARA members visited Elohim City, and funds from the proceeds of their bank robberies made their way into the City of God.

Members of the ARA, working in groups, were responsible for robbing at least 22 banks in seven different states from January 1994 to December 1995. The spree led them across the Midwest to Iowa, Nebraska, Missouri, Ohio and Wisconsin. They stole at least $250,000 during their robberies. They robbed banks with a certain flair and even a macabre sense of humor, using diversions such as fake pipe bombs to slow down the police who were pursuing them.

The group often wore disguises, such as jackets with FBI emblems and Santa Claus costumes during a robbery at Christmastime. They once robbed a bank in Des Moines leaving behind an Easter basket with a gold-painted pipe bomb.

The FBI teletypes and various files on the ARA's bank robberies are designated as the BOMBROB case. The Oklahoma City Bombing is designated as the OKBOMB case in all FBI, ATF and other federal government investigative files. Within days of the Murrah Federal Building bombing, the FBI began investigating links between the ARA and the Oklahoma City Bombing. FBI records demonstrating this fact were hidden by the FBI and not discovered until years later, when attorney Jesse Trentadue uncovered them.

The end of the ARA bank robbery spree came with the arrest of its members after Shawn Kenny had been enlisted as an FBI informant. He had been under surveillance as early as December 1993, according to a Secret Service report. Agents looking for Guthrie noted he had stayed "with Shawn Kenny, Miamitown, Ohio, when in Cincinnati, Ohio area." A search of Kenny's mobile home in December of that year turned up some other interesting items. "It is noted that Kenny has a full library of survivalist and Aryan type literature and admits to being a member of the Aryan Nations and the Christian Identity movement," the report noted. It also stated: "Kenny advised he owned several weapons which were observed to include a high-powered rifle and a 9mm semi-automatic handgun." It is unknown why no weapons charges were brought against Kenny. He had previously been convicted of a gun-related crime, and convicted felons cannot legally own firearms.

In early 1994 Tabatha Kenny, Shawn's wife, contacted a Cincinnati police officer to arrange his arrest for firearms possession and for possessing fraudulent IDs. After his arrest in Hamilton County, Ohio, the files mysteriously disappeared, and there was no record of the arrest anywhere in the system. This could indicate that Kenny was working as an informant for law enforcement as early as the spring of 1994. Timothy McVeigh had several interactions with Kenny during this period.

Despite having been convicted of weapons charges and being a convicted felon, Kenny was sworn into the Army on February 5, 1995. His next run-in with the law came in October 1995. Kenny was once again busted on weapons charges, and he agreed to become an FBI informant and to help capture Wild Bill Guthrie. He agreed to arrange a meeting with Guthrie. It has never been explained how Kenny, with his history of anti-government views, felony convictions and on-going criminal activities, was allowed to remain in the Army. The FBI insists that Kenny "voluntarily" assisted them in capturing Guthrie.

After a meeting between Guthrie and Kenny on January 15, 1996, Guthrie was arrested following a brief car chase through Green Township, a Cincinnati suburb. A Cincinnati police intelligence report dated February 2, 1996, states: "In late 1995, the FBI began working with an informant in an attempt to locate either or both subjects (Guthrie and Langan). Kenny later testified he had cooperated with agents because "just to, I don't know, get this chapter of my life closed and behind me."

Soon after his arrest, Guthrie also turned government snitch and informed federal agents where they could find Peter Langan at an ARA safe house in Columbus, Ohio. On January 18, 1996, a cadre of state, local and federal law enforcement officers and agents set out to arrest Langan. As he sat in his van warming up the engine, at least 47 shots were fired at Langan. It must have been a shock to all that he survived the barrage of bullets fired from rifles, shotguns and pistols. As the smoke cleared from the area, Langan was yanked from the van, thrown to the snow-covered ground, beaten, kicked and restrained by the agents on scene. Medics cut away his clothing and treated his gunshot wounds before transporting him to a local hospital where he underwent surgery for those injuries. Langan was then taken to a local police station and chained to a wall, where FBI Special Agent Ed Woods questioned him. Langan claims that he repeatedly requested a lawyer, but that his pleas were denied.

In a sworn statement provided by Langan on April 9, 2007, he stated: "Instead of obtaining an attorney for me, Agent Woods insisted on playing phone messages from Guthrie's answering machine on a tape recorder. When Agent Woods taunted me with inferences that my associates had betrayed me, and would testify against me, I had had enough. I told him, 'You're going to have problems with your witnesses because they have the blood of Oklahoma City on their hands.' Agent Woods took note. 'You certainly have my attention now,' he said. This turn of events put an end to the interrogation."

Subsequently, Langan's attorney Kevin Dirkin informed his client that the "government wanted to talk to (him) about the Oklahoma City Bombing," according to Langan's statement. Attorney Dirkin referred to this as a proffer or prelude to a plea agreement. In his statement, Langan said: "I was amicable to such a discussion, but I wanted assurances of the terms or details of any type of deal. My attorney later told me the offer had been withdrawn."

Following Guthrie's and Langan's arrests, law enforcement agents uncovered a stockpile of weapons, bombs, bomb-making equipment, fake IDs, U.S. Marshal identification photo IDs and badges, police scanners, money, calling cards, handcuffs, Aryan Nations books, disguises, wigs, masks, false documents and a videotape made by the ARA in January 1995. These items, along with others, were seized from Langan's and Guthrie's vehicles, homes and storage lockers in several different locations.

The ARA videotape, titled *Aryan Republican Army: Armed Struggle Underground*, was made by Guthrie, Langan, McCarthy and Stedeford. According to Guthrie's statements to the FBI, this was the idea of Langan, who wore a disguise and used the alias Commander Pedro. The tape was intended to be a recruitment tape and spelled out the ARA's activities, including their robberies. Langan tells about the ARA and how the group intended to commit an underground struggle to form an Aryan Republic in North America. He speaks of creating cells that would act individually to wage war against the "Zionist Occupied Government." Langan points to a poster that contains the ARA's hit list – including pictures of Attorney General Janet Reno, FBI Director Louis Freeh, President Bill Clinton and Senator Howard Metzenbaum. Langan then states that those pictured already have death sentences passed against them or have been banished by military tribunal. He also makes mention in the video of his "Serb brothers" and their battle for "ethnic cleansing."

Later in the video, the other three ARA members – Guthrie, McCarthy and Stedeford –all wearing Halloween masks, can be seen in the background while Langan asks viewers to work for the revolution and to adhere to the program of Christian Identity. At another point in the video, Langan asks the other members if they are ready for the "courthouse massacre." One member answers in the affirmative, displays a semi-automatic handgun and says there will be many Congressmen and judges there. Langan also proclaims: "We have endeavored to keep collateral damage to a minimum. But as in all wars, some innocents shall suffer. So be it."

"Collateral damage." Timothy McVeigh used that very phrase to refer to the children killed in the Murrah Federal Building.

The ARA's roadmap to forming their Aryan Republic borrowed heavily from the Irish Republican Army. Langan explains that bank robberies are an appropriate way to finance the ARA's revolution because: "Hymie has been ripping you and your father off, forever. Now you go take it back."

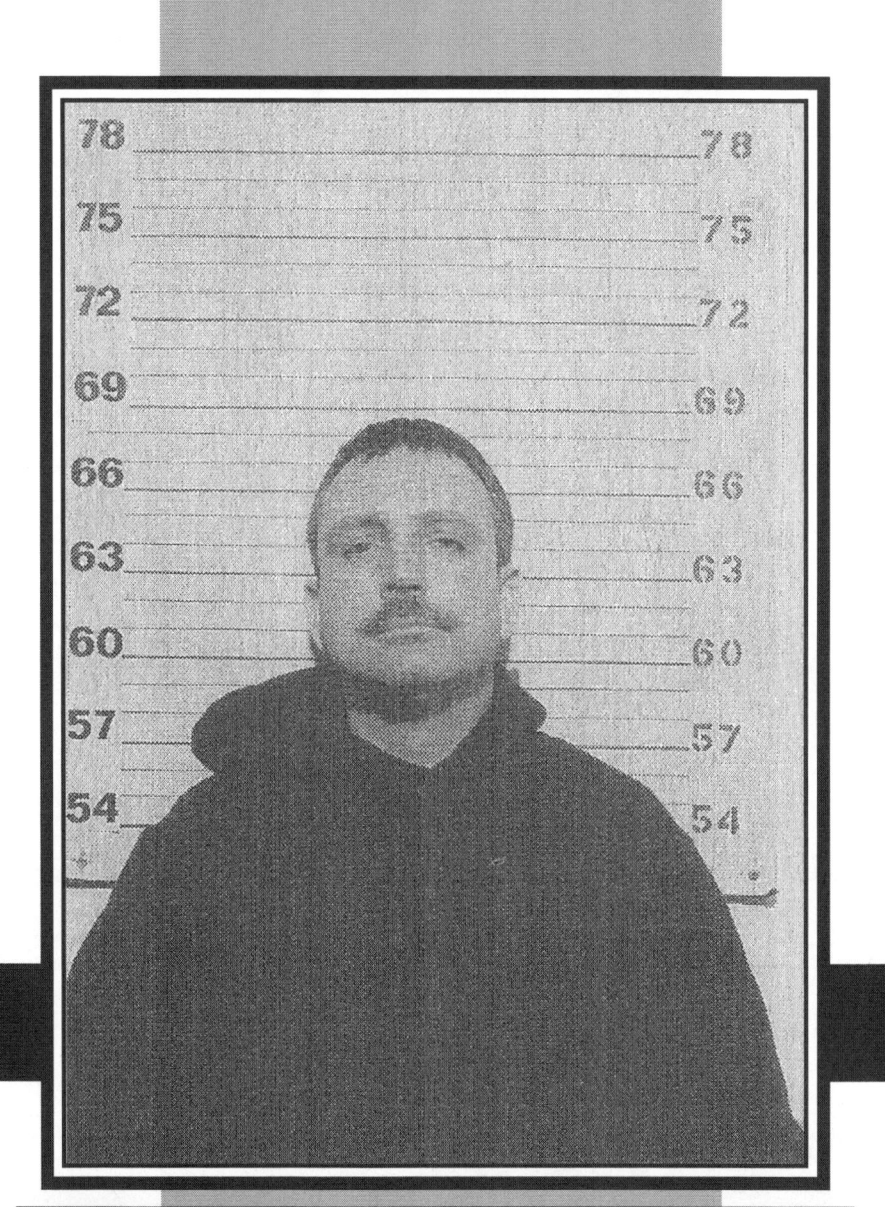

Richard Guthrie

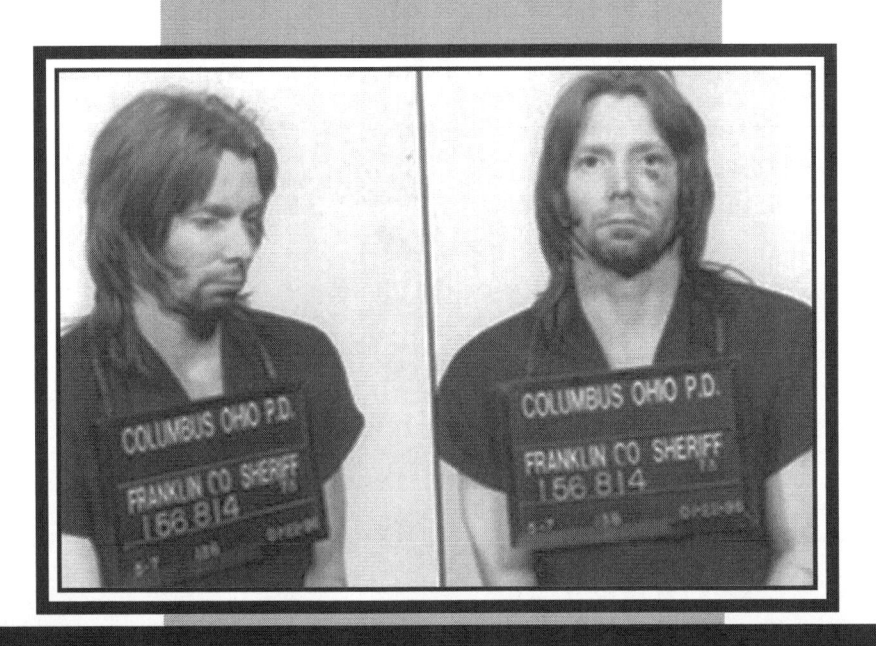

Peter Langan

Michael Brescia

Shawn Kenny

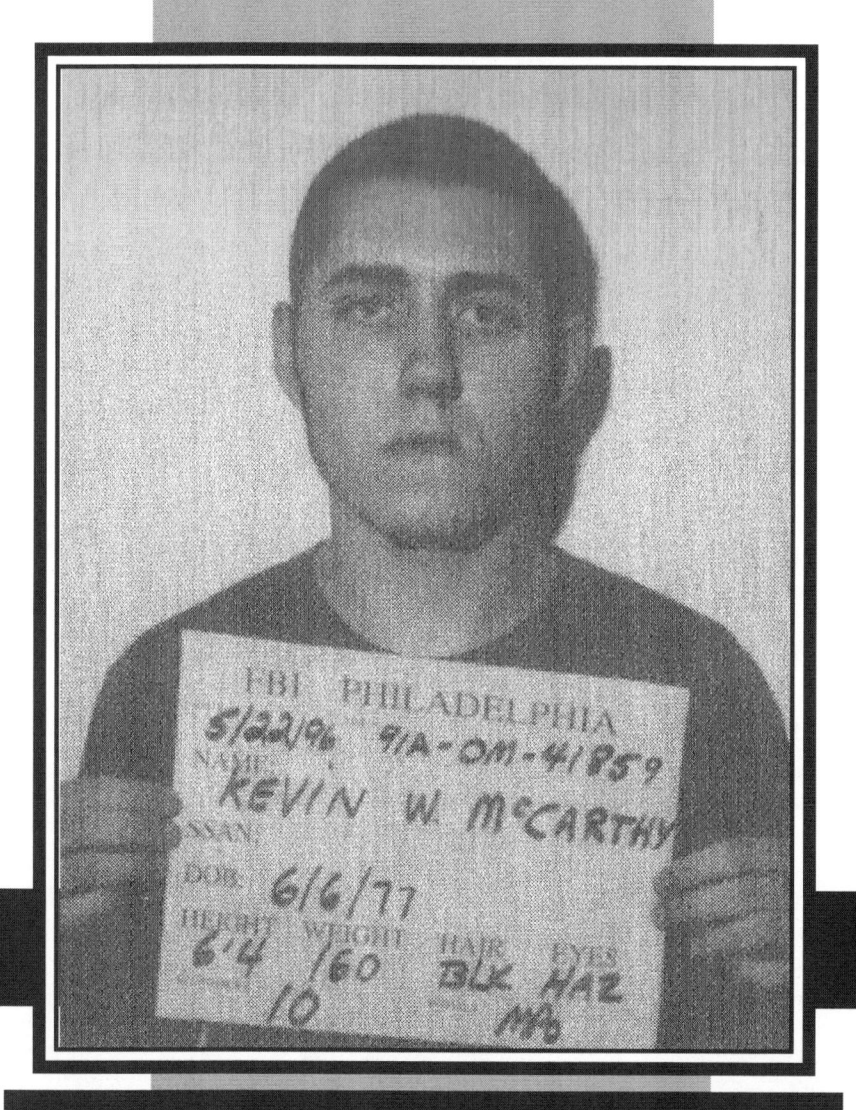

Kevin McCarthy

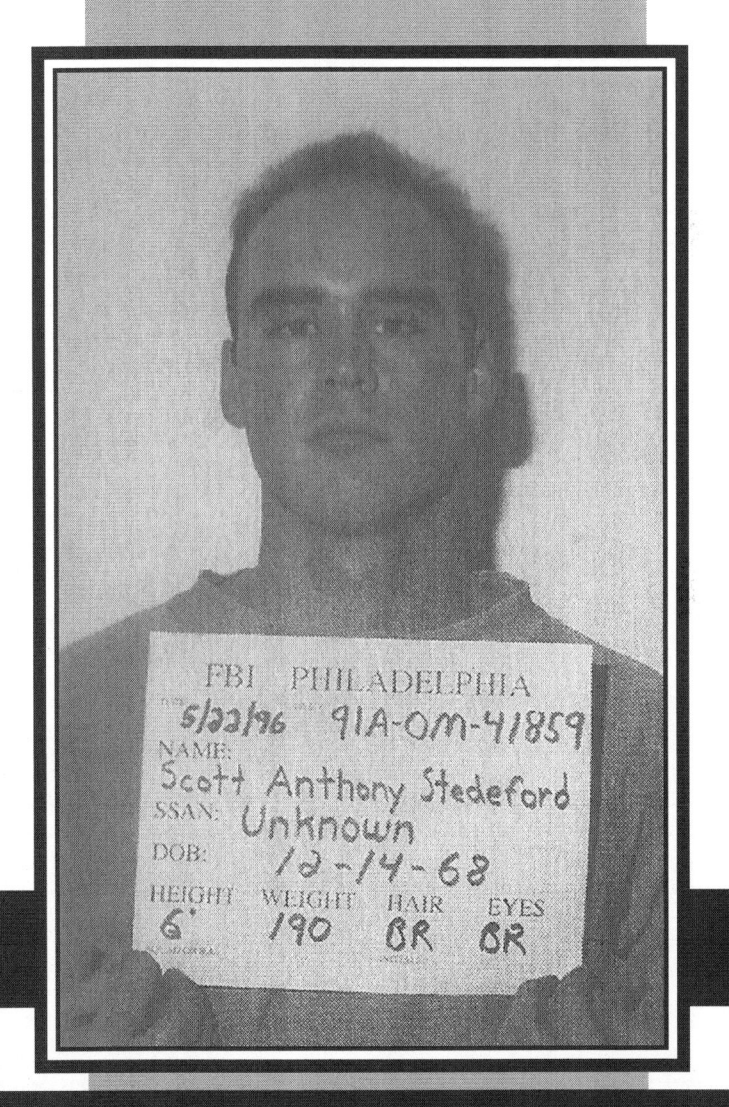

Scott Stedeford

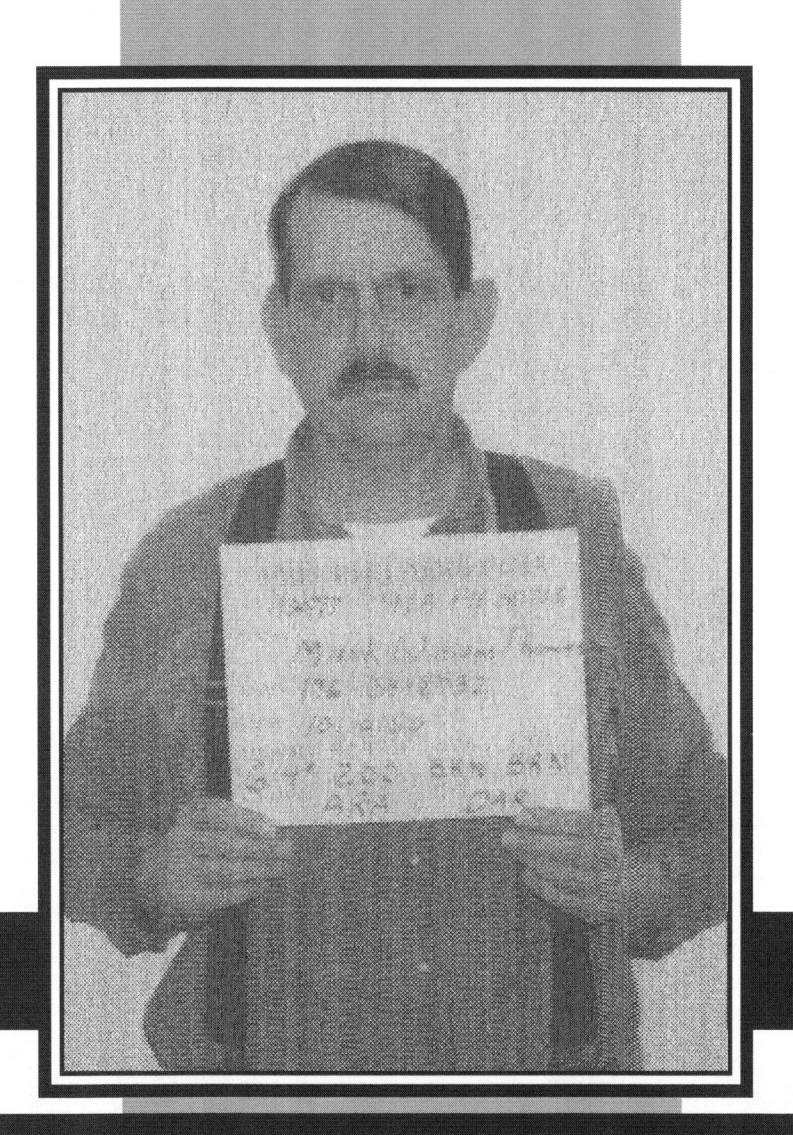

Mark Thomas

After his arrest, Wild Bill Guthrie spent days being interviewed by the FBI and other government officials from the Justice Department. The ARA had been given a security designation as a domestic terrorist group that was a threat to the United States government. In one of his interviews with the FBI, Guthrie claimed that the ARA video had been prepared in a humorous way, but the tape was serious in its message: to eliminate the government currently in place, to eliminate the Jews, and to repatriate all the lands back to white people.

The FBI clearly considered the ARA as a threat. The FBI documents Jesse Trentadue has uncovered relating to the ARA and its connections to McVeigh and the bombing are heavily redacted, but quite revealing. Some reports begin and end with this ominous caution: "Armed and Dangerous: ARA members advocate the violent overthrow of the U.S. Government; are known to be well armed; use explosives; and in the past have fired weapons at agents in an effort to avoid capture."

By 1997, all of the ARA gang members were under arrest.

On May 22, 1996, Scott Stedeford was arrested by the FBI in Upper Darby, Pennsylvania. He was carrying a briefcase that contained a loaded 9mm Ruger semi-automatic handgun, various writings authored by Mark Thomas, a notebook containing code names and phone numbers for unknown individuals and radio frequencies for numerous federal agencies, including the FBI, DEA and ATF. Stedeford refused to be interviewed.

On the same day, Kevin McCarthy was arrested by the FBI at his grandmother's house. He immediately began cooperating with the FBI, spilling his guts about the ARA's involvement in bank robberies and its intent to overthrow the U.S. government. McCarthy immediately agreed to become a government witness against the other ARA members. The government would certainly need McCarthy because their other star witness, Richard Lee Guthrie, would be found dead in his Kenton County, Kentucky jail cell on July 12, 1996. His death was ruled a suicide by hanging, but the circumstances were suspicious. He was a U.S. Marshals Service prisoner being housed in protective custody and confined to an isolation cell.

In 1997, Mark Thomas and Michael Brescia were arrested separately. In a news conference of sorts, Thomas told a crowd of reporters that McCarthy had been involved in the Oklahoma City Bombing. Thomas attributed his knowledge to a statement by Richard Guthrie, who is alleged to have said about McCarthy: "Your young Mr. Wizard took out the Murrah Building." Thomas had once tutored McCarthy in Christian Identity at Thomas' Pennsylvania farm, before McCarthy moved to Elohim City. It was Thomas who had recruited McCarthy into the ARA for the purpose of robbing banks.

This statement by Thomas and the public way he had announced it presented the government with a real problem. Federal prosecutors in Philadelphia were relying on McCarthy's testimony to obtain convictions against Langan and other ARA members. Now the feds cut a deal with Thomas in order to silence him. He entered into a plea agreement and became a government witness. The U.S. attorney prosecuting the ARA case appeared at a press conference and announced that Thomas had recanted his statement about McCarthy and that the story had been concocted to get back at McCarthy. Of course, Guthrie's death prevented him from being able to clear up the matter. Unknown to the media at that time, Guthrie may have spoken from the grave because he did leave behind a manuscript relating to the ARA's exploits. In the manuscript, Guthrie mentioned a mysterious getaway driver named "Tim," also known as "Speedy."

Another connection to McVeigh?

The ARA members who were prosecuted or entered into plea agreements with federal prosecutors were each sentenced to prison for their involvement in bank robberies and/or other related charges. At age 39, Peter Kevin Langan was sentenced to life without the possibility of parole. At age 38, Richard Guthrie, pleaded guilty to 19 bank robberies and cooperated with the FBI before his death. He was expected to receive a 30-year sentence in exchange for his cooperation. At age 47, Mark Thomas, the Pennsylvania state leader of the Aryan Nations, who recruited Scott Stedeford, Kevin McCarthy and Michael Brescia into the ARA, was sentenced to a term of just eight years. Stedeford, 29, was sentenced to a term of 30 years for his involvement in the ARA bank robberies. He is currently housed in a federal prison in Pennsylvania with a release date in 2022. Brescia, 25 at the time of his sentencing, received a term of five years for bank robbery. McCarthy, 20, was also sentenced to five years in prison. Thomas, Brescia and McCarthy have all been released from prison. McCarthy and Thomas remain in the U.S.

Marshal's witness protection program. Langan remains in a maximum-security federal prison serving life. His appeals have been denied, and he has now come forward with information linking some ARA members to the Oklahoma City bombing. However, Langan insists he had no involvement or knowledge of the bombing prior to the event.

Shawn Kenny was never charged or prosecuted for the ARA bank robberies. In a 2004 article published in the *Cincinnati City Beat*, it was reported that Kenny's criminal actions continued while he remained in the Army. Several factors relating to Kenny's acceptance into the U.S. military bear mentioning here. His right-wing political views were readily visible when he testified in court and pointed to the tattoos on his arms. He called one a "crucified skinhead;" the second a "totem kopf," German for "death head." Under the skull is tattooed "SS," the initials for Hitler's storm troopers. U.S. military regulations prohibit recruits who have tattoos of a racist nature.

Even more disturbing is that in March 1996, shortly after Kenny had become an FBI informant and cooperating government witness, he was formally charged with assault under Article 128 of the Uniform Code of Military Justice, and with indecent acts and liberties with a child, Article 134. Kenny provided alcohol to his 11-year-old niece, and inappropriately touched, fondled and kissed her. He served a short administrative suspension and sentence in an Article 15 proceeding. But he was promoted despite his conduct. The Army usually discharges such individuals for such behavior. Kenny's actions took place during his regular stint in the Army. In 2002, after completing his active duty years, he entered the Army National Guard, and in 2004 was promoted to the rank of E-7. He was deployed to Germany for training and then on to Kosovo in 2004. He held the position as a mortar section sergeant. Considering Kenny's associations with the ARA and with Timothy McVeigh, the question arises: Why would the U.S. government train him in the area of explosives?

In his 2007 statement, Peter Langan notes that: "Although involved in the robberies, Shawn Kenny was not prosecuted." Again why?

The strikingly divergent punishments received by the ARA gang members seems to suggest that another factor, the bombing case, may have played a role as these criminals bargained one by one with federal prosecutors – or, in the case of Stedeford, chose not to bargain, or, in Langan's case, failed to come to terms.

If McVeigh's account of the bombing is true, the ARA members who cut deals and got light sentences in the bank robbery case – Thomas, McCarthy, Brescia – had heavy liability in the bomb plot.

In contrast, Stedeford, who refused to cut a deal, got a long prison sentence, just about the norm for serious bank robbery charges.

Guthrie's death, coming as it did just days after he told a reporter he was going to "blow the lid off" the bombing case, suggests he had culpability, that the bombing may have figured in his plea bargain, and that may have caused him remorse.

An affidavit by former Cincinnati police officer Matthew Moning goes further. According to Moning, a federal agent told him that Guthrie "committed suicide after being told he was going to be executed for his role in the Oklahoma City Bombing case. He was told that money from his robberies had been tied to that case and that that meant the death sentence."

Langan's fate still hangs in the balance, as he continues, so far unsuccessfully, to try to use his information against others to lighten his sentence.

As for Shawn Kenny, his case practically smells of a deal. Kenny was rewarded to the maximum, perhaps, for facilitating the arrest of Guthrie, evidently the prize catch in the bank robbery case. But the fact that Kenny escaped all charges in several serious criminal scenarios where there was compelling evidence against him, and even was rewarded with Army promotions, suggests he might have extraordinary leverage with the government. But what?

7

CHAPTER SEVEN

ANDY THE GERMAN

Andreas Carl Strassmeir was born on May 17, 1959, in Germany to a prominent family with political connections. To this day there is much about Strassmeir, also known as Andy the German and Mr. Red, that remains a mystery. His story has been told in great books such as *The Secret Life of Bill Clinton*, by Ambrose Evans-Pritchard; *In Bad Company*, by Mark Hamm; and *Others Unknown*, by Stephen Jones. Investigative reporter J.D. Cash, now deceased, provided me with much of the background on Strassmeir that is contained herein.

Strassmeir is the son of Gunter Strassmeir, former Parliamentary Secretary of State to German Chancellor Helmut Kohl. Andreas's uncle was in the German Parliament, and his brother Alexander was on the Berlin City Council. Strassmeir's father also is reported to have ties to the CIA.

Andreas Strassmeir served as a lieutenant in the Panzer Grenadiers, the German equivalent of U.S. Special Forces. As an officer, he received advanced training at a military academy in Hamburg. That schooling included intelligence training. One of his military assignments included a stint as a liaison officer with the Welsh Guards. In an interview with the *London Sunday Telegraph*, Strassmeir stated that part of his work was to detect infiltration by foreign agents and then feed them disinformation. "If we caught a guy, we'd offer him amnesty," Strassmeir said. " We'd turn him and use him to feed false information back to the Warsaw Pact." It was widely believed that Strassmeir was an agent for the German anti-terrorist unit, the GSG-9.

The exact reasons why Andreas Strassmeir came to the United States may never be known, but some things have been verified. He came here in the late 1980s with others, for the stated purpose of participating in a re-enactment of the Battle of Gettysburg. He was equipped with authentic period uniforms and was very knowledgeable about the battle. During his visit, Vincent Petruskie, a retired U.S. Air Force colonel, provided him hospitality. Strassmeir told the *Telegraph* during a five-part interview that he came to the U.S. in 1989 to work on a "special assignment" for the Justice Department. "I discussed the job when I was in Washington," he said. " I was hoping to work for the operations section of the DEA [Drug Enforcement Administration]. But it never worked out."

Strassmeir also informed attorney Mike Johnston during an interview in Berlin that Petruski is "a former CIA guy who my father had known since he (Petruski) was stationed in Berlin during the Cold War." Pertuski has denied any connection to the CIA. He was interviewed by the editor of *New American* and stated that as for any CIA connection: "That's totally wrong. . . I'm a retired Air Force officer, that's all." Petruski did admit to having been a special agent with the Air Force Office of Special Investigations. He served in the Air Force from 1954 to 1975. When asked if he was a friend of Strassmeir's father, Petruski replied: "I've never met his father; we've only spoken over the phone."

According to Petruski: Strassmeir was "a mixed up kid, a very immature 34-year-old when he came over here. Andy wanted to work for the U.S. government, DEA, Justice – undercover. [He] thought his background with military and German government would help. I explained he'd need a green card, education, and sat him down with some people in Washington who explained that it wasn't that simple."

Apparently the job never materialized, or did it?

It is far more likely, considering events that followed, that the Gettysburg story was nothing more than a cover story, which Strassmeir would use as he set out to infiltrate the right-wing movement in the U.S. Petruski told Cash that Strassmeir "is what we would call a putz." Cash wasn't buying that claim. His own investigation told a far different story. There was far more to Andy the German than the portrait Petruski was trying to sell as he attempted to distance himself from Strassmeir. Cash's journalistic instincts were exceptional. He could smell a con job from a mile away. Petruski's tale about the DEA job not panning out for the son of his German friend didn't cover jobs for other government agencies such as the FBI or ATF. Strassmeir clearly had an agenda. According to Petruski's statements to Cash: "He [Andreas] went down to North or South Carolina and then to Texas. He was going to school down there."

There are FBI records that reveal Strassmeir's presence in Texas in 1989 and 1991. FBI interview statements obtained by online journalist J.M. Berger, who publishes *INTELWIRE.com,* establish that Strassmeir was a member of the Texas Reserve Militia, also known as the Texas Light Infantry Militia, for several years. Those documents also verify that there were no fewer than four separate FBI informants and three FBI agents inside the TRM simultaneously with the group's membership of 15-50 members during the same time period. The TRM members suspected that Strassmeir was an informant after they followed him to a federal building at night and observed him entering the building after punching a code into a keypad.

According to a statement made by Strassmeir in February 1996, he admitted to residing at Elohim City. "I was at Elohim City on and off for about four years, from 1991 until August of 1995," he said.

Strassmeir also admitted to being a training instructor for those involved in providing security at Elohim City. He denied being the chief of security. He claimed his history in the military landed him the training position at Elohim City, and he became involved in the security patrol that had been in place upon his arrival. Contrary to his claims, it is a documented fact that regardless of his title, Andy the German, as he was known by those he trained at the Elohim City compound, was in charge of all things weapons-related.

The Oklahoma State Bureau of Investigation has reported that Strassmeir was responsible for training platoon-sized groups consisting of 30-40 individuals from across the country, every three months or so. In Strassmeir's statement he claimed that an elder at Elohim City, Azara Patterson, a former Marine, always held the position of chief of security at the compound.

According to Patterson, in an interview with J.D. Cash published in the *McCurtain Gazette*: "Strassmeir went out and replaced all our deer rifles with assault weapons . . . Next, he wanted us to start doing illegal stuff . . . a lot of illegal stuff. I kept telling Andy that we were defensive here, and we didn't want any problems with the law."

Andy the German conducted paramilitary training and drills for residents and visitors. Many young men in various right-wing groups such as skinheads, KKK, and WAR traveled to Elohim City specifically to train under Strassmeir. The ARA members went to Elohim City, and at least three of them – Brescia, McCarthy and Stedeford – trained under Andy the German. They all three were his roommates, and Brescia became his assistant.

Strassmeir's stay at Elohim City was not without interruptions and run-ins with law enforcement. On February 28, 1992, he was arrested, and the Oklahoma State Highway Patrol impounded his car. According to Kenny Pence, the tow-truck driver, Strassmeir ran a roadblock and presented a driver's license belonging to Elohim City resident Peter Ward. Trooper Vernon Phillips instructed Pence to tow the vehicle, an old, burgundy-colored station wagon. The state placed a hold on the car because of "tag or taxes . . . or something;" Pence did not specifically recall what. He did, however, remember inventorying the vehicle with the trooper and finding some "strange documents" written in German. According to a statement provided by Pence to McVeigh's defense team on September 5, 1996, Phillips never got a chance to follow up on the documents because "the car got released so quickly." Pence received a phone call stating that Strassmeir had diplomatic immunity. There was some confusion over who owned the vehicle. The owner was said to be Peter Ward, but papers inside the car seemed to indicate it was Strassmeir's.

What is clear is that within the span of a couple of hours, Pence received telephone calls from the State Department, from a military base in North or South Carolina, and from attorney Kirk Lyons, who has represented high-profile white supremacists. Eventually Pence received a call from someone in the Oklahoma Department of Public

Safety, who instructed Pence to release the vehicle to Strassmeir. Pence was told that the Governor's office had become involved. He made adjustments to the towing bill and waited for Strassmeir to retrieve the car. According to Pence, Andy the German arrived clothed in a full-length black coat and spoke with a heavy German accent, which startled Pence. He said that Strassmeir was friendly until he discovered that his papers had been rummaged through and that he "just had an absolute fit." Pence couldn't understand what the guy was saying, but he was furious. Pence explained to Strassmeir that everything in an impounded vehicle is always inventoried carefully in order to protect the belongings of the vehicle owner. He also commented that Strassmeir must have a lot of pull somewhere and he thought it was a "really strange deal."

Strassmeir must have decided he needed a driver's license of his own because on August 28, 1992, he received a driver's license issued by the State of Tennessee. He listed his address as 7613 Thorngrove Pike, Knoxville. Even stranger is that Strassmeir had an active social security number despite being in the United States illegally.

As for his association with Timothy McVeigh, Strassmeir has had remarkably little to say, and nothing about McVeigh in Elohim City. In his February 1996 statement, Strassmeir acknowledged he traveled the gun show circuit in Oklahoma and Arkansas to buy, trade and sell "materials." He admitted to having met Timothy McVeigh, but claimed to have forgotten all about it until McVeigh's defense attorney interviewed him.

What is known is that during the months in which McVeigh said Strassmeir was helping plan the bombing, informant Carol Howe's ATF handler was becoming increasingly alarmed by reports on Strassmeir's activities. In 1992, he had supervised the building of bunkers and a weapons storage facility on the Elohim City compound. Now, in early 1995, ATF Agent Finley-Graham had aerial surveillance photographs of Strassmeir with an assault weapon and of the bunkers. On February 7, 1995, the Oklahoma Highway Patrol was flying photo recon over Elohim City at the request of the ATF. The threat level at Elohim City had reached a point at which the ATF in Tulsa had decided to seek arrest warrants for Strassmeir, Dennis Mahon and others. These facts are contained in Finley-Graham's reports.

This was the beginning of Strassmeir's near arrest. The ATF had clear and convincing evidence against him for conspiracy and weapons violations. The INS had violations against him for being an illegal alien. In mid-February, the ATF issued a Be On The Lookout bulletin for Strassmeir. The BOLO stated:

> Andreas Strassmeir, W/M, 5/17/59, heavy German accent. Black Hair/Blue eyes. 1" scar on chin, wears cammo fatigues. Possible Tennessee Driver's license. Came to USA in 5/91, passport was good until 8/91. He never left the country. The INS says he does not have an extension of his VISA. Possibly in blue Chevy, late model, tag BSH 346 (not on file), usually has someone driving for him. Carries a .45 auto pistol at all times. He is an illegal alien, ATF wants to be notified if he is stopped and has the gun on him. They will file charges. Contact: Agent Angela Findley, ATF Office.

But the arrest never happened. For reasons that still remain unknown, a planned ATF and INS joint raid on Elohim City was stopped in its tracks in February 1995, at the direction of FBI Special Agent in Charge, Bob Ricks, of the Oklahoma City office.

This was extremely puzzling. How could this happen? The most plausible explanation would seem to be that Strassmeir was an agent or confidential informant, protected from prosecution. The question is: to whom was he reporting? Was it the FBI, CIA, or ATF? Or was Strassmeir attached to one of the Major's special units?

Strassmeir fled Elohim City for North Carolina in August 1995, four months after the bombing, when the spotlight began to shine too brightly on Elohim City, and the neo-Nazis who stayed and trained there. On July 14, 1996, six months to the day after Strassmeir had been smuggled out of the United States by way of Mexico, J.D. Cash wrote in the *McCurtain Gazette* that a highly placed FBI official had confirmed that Andreas Strassmeir was a paid government informant sent by ATF – the same agency that employed Carol Howe – to infiltrate Elohim City.

In an interview with the *London Sunday Telegraph*, Strassmeir played it just a bit too cool when he all but admitted that he was undercover

Deadly Secrets

while in the U.S. "The Right-wing in the U.S. is incredibly easy to penetrate if you know how to talk to them," Strassmeir said. He added: "Of course, it's easier for a foreigner with an accent; nobody would ever suspect a German of working for the Federal Government." But some did suspect just that.

8

CHAPTER EIGHT

ROGER MOORE

In Timothy McVeigh's statements to me, he never indicated that Roger Moore had been anything other than what he seemed: a friendly presence on the gun-show circuit, a like-minded associate who became a useful friend and sometimes host, until, according to McVeigh, Strassmeir and McVeigh targeted Moore for robbery.

If McVeigh had any idea that Roger Moore was a government agent, he never told me, or even dropped a hint. But stunning information to that effect comes from another source. Attorney Jesse Trentadue interviewed McVeigh's convicted accomplice, Terry Nichols, face to face in ADX Supermax prison in 2007.

Nichols had been trying to tell this story to someone ever since 2004, when he was convicted a second time in state court for the bombing, and received a life sentence. But when Nichols wrote then-Attorney Gen. Ashcroft and offered to tell his story, Ashcroft didn't even answer the letter. More roadblocks followed, including a ban on all media interviews with Nichols. But Trentadue, who had been investigating the bombing case for several years, wanted to hear Nichols' story, and visited him at Supermax as a lawyer.

Then and there, Terry Nichols broke his long silence about the crime. Nichols told Trentadue he knew Timothy McVeigh was an undercover agent in a sting operation, because McVeigh told him so.

Nichols also told Trentadue that he knew Roger Moore was not the robbery victim he seemed to be, but actually a player in the bomb plot, again because McVeigh told him so. According to Nichols, McVeigh said he and Moore came up with the idea of doing a staged robbery at Moore's home, which would provide money for McVeigh's mission. Later, after studying the case further, Nichols came to the conclusion that Roger Moore's role went deeper than McVeigh knew. Nichols now believes Moore was actually operating as an "agent provocateur" under instructions from someone else who was running the sting. The Major, perhaps?

"The truth is Roger Moore is being protected because by revealing the truth it will <u>implicate</u> the federal government (our own gov't) in the OKC bombing!!" Nichols has written.

Terry Nichols is no fool. Sitting in Supermax, he knew his status as convicted murderer would present serious credibility problems for his story. He didn't expect Jesse Trentadue to take him at his word. To support his allegations about Moore, Nichols handed over a thick investigative file. Sitting in isolation in his prison cell for several years, Nichols had pored over his memories, investigative files compiled by his defense teams and, in some cases, the FBI.

The file Nichols turned over to Trentadue paints a damaging picture of Roger Moore, one likely to leave a reader wondering – as in the cases of Shawn Kenny and Andreas Strassmeir – why this man was apparently never investigated in connection with the Oklahoma City Bombing. I have drawn extensively on the Terry Nichols file for the following summary profile.

Roger Edwin Moore was born on December 20, 1934. He was raised in Sioux City, Iowa, and attended school there. After graduating from high school he joined the Air Force where he served for seven years, obtaining the rank of armament sergeant. He was also captain of the rifle team. He married his wife Carol in May of 1955.

Moore attended the University of Tulsa, where he earned a Master's Degree in Business Management. While attending graduate school he worked for North American Aviation, now Rockwell International, as a manager in the engineering department with a government Top Secret clearance. After living in Tulsa for several years, the Moores moved to Florida, where they resided for the next 20 years.

In Florida, Moore became involved in the boat business, selling 36-foot fiberglass boats. The Navy in Vietnam used some of these boats as patrol boats. He also built boats for elite customers who used them for ocean racing. He owned a total of five boat-building companies from 1966 until about 1977, when he sold his businesses and property. The last two companies owned by Moore were Ensign Marine Inc. and Trophy Marine Inc., based in Fort Lauderdale. They were large enough to be publicly traded.

Roger Moore and his wife Carol made a tremendous profit off the sale of the businesses, which enabled them to live off the proceeds via investments. Subsequently, Moore began to travel extensively throughout the country looking to establish a ranch. By the 1990s, when he knew Timothy McVeigh, Moore was living for part of the year on his ranch in Royal, Arkansas, with his girlfriend Karen Anderson.

Moore met Anderson in 1979 in Fort Lauderdale. They moved to Arkansas several years later. Moore divided his time between the Arkansas ranch and his home in Florida. Anderson was a professional horsewoman and has held a world equestrian title in jumping. She has more recently operated two businesses with Moore, called the American Assault Company and the Candy Store. Karen Anderson has a federal firearms license in the name of Kathy Anderson. Moore does not hold any such license. Their businesses sold ammunition and parts for firearms, at least on the surface. They also sold adult videos.

While residing together in Arkansas, Moore and Anderson had some misfortunes that included a theft on August 11, 1986. Their housekeeper, Patricia R. Ciactello, allegedly stole $11,000 in cash and fled the ranch while Moore and Anderson were in town. The Garland County Sheriff's Department issued a warrant for her arrest. Ciacatello was never arrested for the theft. She was alleged to have committed suicide eight years later in Apache Junction, Arizona, near Phoenix, on April 14, 1994. Timothy McVeigh told me he killed this woman as a favor for Roger Moore.

On October 10, 1986, Layton Noel, a friend of Moore and Anderson who was staying at their ranch, reportedly committed suicide in their garage while they were on a weekend trip to Tulsa. His cause of death was determined to be carbon monoxide poisoning by the Garland County, Arkansas coroner, who investigated the death.

The ATF and Arkansas State Police investigated Moore and Anderson in 1989. The police received information from a confidential informant in Florida that Robert Miller (the alias used by Moore at gun shows to protect his real identity) was willing to illegally send hundreds of pounds of C-4 explosives via UPS from Arkansas to Florida. The Garland County Prosecuting Attorney's Office issued a subpoena in May 1989 in order to investigate Moore and Anderson. An ATF special agent was supposed to have his confidential informant in Florida attempt to contact Roger Moore to arrange a shipment of the explosives. But that never happened. The case was closed on May 4, 1989, without any explanation. According to reporter J.D. Cash, Roger Moore agreed to become an ATF informant at that time.

Surprisingly, even while Moore was apparently acting as an ATF informant, the Arkansas State Police and the ATF again investigated Moore and Anderson in March 1993, this time for selling illegal weapons via the mail to a convicted felon, Ron Goldberg of Oregon. But an FBI special agent from the Hot Springs, Arkansas, office advised that there were no weapons violations of Karen Anderson's federal firearms license privileges. Therefore, the case was closed.

During this same time period, Anderson and Moore were dealing with Steven Colbern, who was a federal fugitive. Anderson sold Colbern .50 and .308 caliber ammunition by mail. Astoundingly, it was Anderson who now took it upon herself to personally introduce Colbern to Timothy McVeigh. Following Anderson's introduction, McVeigh and Colbern became friends, and, according to McVeigh, conducted bomb-making experiments in the summer of 1994 in the Arizona desert near Kingman.

No charges were ever filed against Anderson or Moore over their weapons and ammunition dealings with convicted felons Goldberg and Colbern, or for any other state or federal offenses. Like many persons associated with Timothy McVeigh, Moore and Anderson seem to have been protected from prosecution.

Deadly Secrets

Terry Nichols

When the FBI first questioned Anderson about McVeigh and Colbern on May 5, 1995, Anderson claimed not to know Colbern. However, when questioned by the FBI a second time two weeks later on May 17, 1995, her memory improved. She now recalled her dealings with Colbern – not just selling him ammunition and introducing him to McVeigh, but also acting as a mail forwarding person for Colbern, so that his real location would not be known. Anderson also stated that her last contact with Colbern came approximately one month before the Oklahoma City Bombing.

A month later, in June 1995, the story of the November 1994 robbery at Roger Moore's Arkansas home broke for the first time, when the FBI released documents related to searches of the homes of McVeigh and Nichols. The *Arkansas Democrat Gazette* published a series of articles focusing on the robbery and Moore. On June 16, after the media reported Moore's name as the robbery victim, Moore said he believed his life was in danger. At a press conference, Garland County Sheriff Larry Selig said: "Moore fears any perception that he may be cooperating in the Oklahoma City bombing investigation." Moore was in seclusion, but a television reporter from Little Rock managed to interview him at the gate to his property. According to the reporter, Moore said he had met with FBI officials almost 30 times since the bombing. Moore later discounted the number 30, but declined to say how many times the FBI had interviewed him.

The big headline in the series – 'Cover' blown – came on June 22, when the newspaper reported on Moore's unsuccessful effort to have the local sheriff's department withhold the robbery report. According to the newspaper, after the report was released over Moore's objection, he made a statement suggesting he was playing or had played some kind of informant role with the FBI. "Whatever I was doing for the FBI is f***** up because they blew my cover," the newspaper quoted Moore as saying.

Another strange episode in which Moore reportedly claimed a relationship with the FBI began in the fall of 1993, when Moore had a run-in with Oklahoma State Highway Patrol troopers. He was arrested for shooting at an occupied vehicle during a traffic stop and for possession of drugs. On November 23, 1993, Moore retained Richard McLaughlin, an attorney in Wagoner, Oklahoma, to represent him.

According to McLaughlin, Moore acted "real snappy and smart" at every court appearance. He was loud and said inappropriate things to the judge, such as, "This is all nonsense." Moore acted as if the charges were the result of a conspiracy among the Oklahoma State Highway Patrol personnel, the District Attorney, the judge, and even McLaughlin himself. Moore lodged a complaint against the state troopers who had arrested him. Moore acted as if he was above the law.

On October 25, 1995, Moore came into McLaughlin's office angry and complaining that the lawyer had overcharged him. During that confrontation, McLaughlin told Moore he hoped the government indicted him for financing the Oklahoma City Bombing. In response, according to McLaughlin, Moore got a funny look on his face and stated they would not do anything because he was a "protected witness."

There it was from Roger Moore's own mouth, just five months after the bombing. He was a protected witness. Apparently, Moore had disclosed enough to his attorney to cause McLaughlin to think Moore might be prosecutable in the bombing case. If Moore was "protected," as he claimed, was it because he had been secretly informing on someone? Timothy McVeigh?

Moore's alleged claim that he was protected seems to have support in various documents that eventually made their way to Terry Nichols for his file. In an FBI interview statement dated February 27, 1996, Special Agent Ronald J. Van Vranken of the Salt Lake City Field Office stated that Utah Assistant U.S. Attorney Bruce Lubeck had declined to prosecute Roger Moore in August 1991, for Moore's alleged involvement in illegal drug activities targeted by Operation Punchout, a federal undercover drug sting.

The reason given on the court-docketing sheet for the failure to prosecute Moore was "insufficient evidence." Unfortunately, Lubeck could not locate his letter declining prosecution of Moore in his files. Time and again Moore seems to have been protected by someone in the federal government.

If Timothy McVeigh believed or knew that Roger Moore was a government agent, McVeigh never told his attorneys. But the defense file does contain one very telling document suggesting that by the time of McVeigh's trial, he harbored resentment toward Moore that suggested their relationship in the bombing conspiracy went well beyond thief and victim.

In December 1995, McVeigh's investigator Richard Reyna met with McVeigh at the federal prison at El Reno. Reyna informed McVeigh that the FBI was increasing the pressure on Moore, "and that it was just a matter of time before Moore decides to cooperate." The investigator also told McVeigh there was no doubt in his mind that "Roger Moore could be a very damaging witness." Reyna went on to say: "I told Mr. McVeigh to wake up and smell the coffee . . . that Mr. Moore was not a stupid man, that if it came down to making a choice about whose ass to save, that McVeigh could kiss his ass goodbye."

According to Reyna, the look on McVeigh's face when the investigator delivered this news was one of anger. In response: "Mr. McVeigh stated that if Moore decided to testify against him, there was enough evidence available to sink Roger Moore." Specifically, McVeigh went on to describe some of the explosives Moore had provided him, including Kinestiks, one of the explosives McVeigh told me were final ingredients in the bomb constructed in the warehouse in Oklahoma City. McVeigh told Reyna that Moore had cases of the explosive Kinestik, but that he didn't sell it to just anybody. McVeigh claimed that Moore was anti-government, and told McVeigh he didn't mind selling the explosives to him because he knew McVeigh would "put them to good use."

In the sworn declaration Terry Nichols gave Jesse Trentadue in 2007, Nichols claimed – contradicting McVeigh, who told me Guthrie and Brescia were the robbers – that he, Nichols, was the one who personally robbed Roger Moore on November 5, 1994. In the declaration, Nichols elaborated on the link between Roger Moore and the Kinestik explosive McVeigh said he used in the bomb. "Among the things that I took from Moore was a box containing tubes of nitromethane, which forms part of the binary explosive Kinestik," Nichols said, adding that: "I hid those explosives at my home after the bombing. Although Moore denies ever having Kinestik, these explosives that I took that day were in a box addressed to Robert Miller, which was Moore's alias. I also have no doubt that Moore's fingerprints are on that box and/or those explosives."

If Jesse Trentadue hadn't followed a long and twisted path of clues all the way to Terry Nichols, everyone might have forgotten about this most intriguing piece of explosive evidence, which is now in the custody of the FBI. After Nichols revealed the whereabouts of the nitromethane, FBI agents raided his home in Herington, Kansas, and found the carton of nitromethane right where Nichols said it would be.

But curiously, no investigative report on the confiscated nitromethane ever issued from the FBI. Trentadue has requested through the Freedom of Information Act all relevant information as to whose fingerprints were found on the box and the explosives. To date his request has not been answered. It is unknown whether the FBI or ATF even bothered to test for prints.

Roger Moore and Karen Anderson have moved from their Arkansas ranch. Moore's actions apparently never aroused the suspicions of the FBI. So far, about the only investigator seriously interested in Roger Moore is a private citizen: Jesse Trentadue.

9

CHAPTER NINE

TRENTADUE BLOOD

Jesse Carl Trentadue doesn't look like any hillbilly one's mind might conjure up. But after years of battling the FBI over release of government secrets about the Oklahoma City Bombing – secrets Jesse believes may finally explain his brother's suspicious death in the summer of 1995 – he is no doubt running out of patience. Maybe that is bringing out the hillbilly in him.

Jesse doesn't wear bibbed overalls, denim work pants, straw hats or caps from the local grain dealership. But his roots run deep into the coal mining camps of West Virginia. His hometown is called, simply, Number 7, West Virginia, a tiny coal mining camp in the hills about halfway between Horsepen, Virginia, and Cucumber, West Virginia. His father went to work in the mine at age 15. His grandfathers on both sides of his family started working in the mines at ages 6 and 12. In addition to coal mining, Jesse's family had another tradition. They served their country in various branches of the U.S. military dating back to the Civil War. Jesse himself served a two-year hitch in the Marine Corps before he enrolled in law school.

Jesse's father and grandfathers all died from black lung disease after a lifetime of working in the mines. Coal prices plummeted during the

Korean War and a neighboring family from Number 7 moved west to Orange County, California. The Lassaks were Trentadue family friends from up the holler. Mr. Lassaks had "prophesied of a promised land in California." In no time at all the locals of Number 7 received word that Mrs. Lassaks was on the TV game show *Queen for a Day,* where the woman with the saddest story would win a crown, a case of Chesterfield cigarettes and a washing machine. According to Jesse, "She told a tragic Number 7 story about living in houses with dirt floors and eating fried potato peels, coons, groundhogs and squirrel, and she broke the applause meter." That was enough proof for the folks in and around Number 7, "and about half the entire damned town moved west to Orange County."

Jesse's own family was one of those that made the trip. "We headed west on ole' Route 66, just like the Okies did," Jesse says. "We slept beside the car at night. We cooked our meals beside the road."

In high school Jesse excelled at sports, but after a football injury he discovered he had another God-given talent. He set the state record in California for being the fastest high-school athlete at running the mile. That feat was good enough to win him a full track and field scholarship at the University of Southern California, where he and his fellow teammate O.J. Simpson made All American. Following graduation, Jesse joined the Marines, served with honor and then attended law school at the University of Idaho. He later moved to Salt Lake City where he earned a reputation as a tough and spirited litigator. He practices law there today. That is, when he's not on the front lines in his role as a tenacious citizen investigator.

Jesse's appearance might fool you. He's often seen wearing a Gatsby cap and smoking on a cigar while chewing tobacco at the same time. His neatly trimmed beard and gray-streaked mustache give the appearance of a modern-day gunslinger. He is stocky, with a weather-beaten look, sharp as a tack, yet reserved and watchful. He shows the strain of the past 15 plus years of seeking justice for his brother, Kenneth Michael Trentadue. Kenney's gruesome death in federal custody in Oklahoma City, four months after the bombing, is what drew Jesse into the spider's web of the bombing case. He has been doggedly investigating to solve what he believes was a murder ever since.

Jesse's younger brother Kenney was also a high school athlete. He had dreams of following in his older brother's footsteps. Jesse was three years older and the two brothers had grown up close, sharing hardships and triumphs. An injury put an end to Kenney's dream of being a distance runner. He dropped out of high school and began hanging around with other boys from their neighborhood. At age 17 he enlisted in the Army. During his stint in the service he became a drug addict. Afterwards he robbed some pharmacies to feed his habit.

Kenney worked at numerous jobs, including carpentry and factory work. He then became a bank robber. He wouldn't just rob the tellers, but took down the whole bank. But as Jesse says: "On Kenney's jobs, the weapons were empty or the firing pins had been removed. Robbery is one thing. Murder is something totally different, and money isn't worth that." Kenney was arrested for the bank robberies. "He didn't cry about it," Jesse says. " He went in, pled guilty, and served his time."

Kenney was released from federal prison in 1987, but remained on parole. He had served six years of a 20-year sentence for robbing a savings and loan. Life on the outside wasn't easy for him, but he cleaned up his act. Kenney got married, bought a home and had steady work in construction. He enjoyed a cold beer after work and lived a law-abiding existence. For some unknown reason, his parole officer instituted a no-alcohol provision to his parole agreement. Kenney appealed the ban, but lost. In protest he stopped reporting to his parole officer. For the next eight years he was a successful member of society. In the spring of 1995, he and his wife Carmen were expecting their first child.

On June 10, 1995, about two months after the Oklahoma City Bombing, Kenney was pulled over at the Mexican border while driving his 1986 Chevy pickup. Kenney was on his way home to San Diego after visiting his in-laws in Mexico. He had made this trip routinely without ever encountering difficulties. This stop was different. As a part of the normal crossing procedures, officials at the border ran a criminal computer check on Kenney Trentadue. The National Crime and Information Center reported the 1987 arrest warrant issued for Kenney's failure to report to his parole officer. He was arrested and transported to the Metropolitan Correctional Center in San Diego. That facility houses federal prisoners temporarily during the adjudication of their charges.

Kenney was a well-muscled, dark haired man, 5'8" and stocky. His left forearm bore a dragon tattoo. He was in top physical shape after years of working in construction. After waiting for two months in MCC San Diego for a parole revocation hearing, he was unexpectedly transported by the U.S. Marshals Service - via Con Air - to the Federal Bureau of Prisons' Federal Transfer Center, located on the edge of Will Rogers World Airport in Oklahoma City. Kenney arrived there on August 18, 1995, as a parole violator who faced no more than three to six months in prison, if his parole was actually revoked. His son Vito had just been born two months earlier, nine days after his arrest at the border.

On August 19, 1995, Kenney placed a telephone call to Jesse's house. Kenney spoke to his sister-in-law Rita. He reported on being flown to Oklahoma City pending a parole revocation hearing. Rita is an attorney and law professor, and she was surprised that Kenney had been shipped from California to Oklahoma for such a hearing. In that conversation he told her: "It's that jet age stuff." Their conversation was routinely recorded by the BOP. Kenney called again that night and spoke with Jesse. "Kenney was in good spirits," Jesse recalls. "We talked about the hearing and he promised to call me back the next night." That call never came.

In the early morning hours of August 21, 1995, FTC-Oklahoma City's Acting Warden Marie Carter placed a telephone call to Jesse's mother Wilma Trentadue. The acting warden informed Mrs. Trentadue that her son Kenney, also known as Vance Paul Brockway (an alias from his bank robbing days) had committed suicide. Acting Warden Carter then offered to have Kenney's body cremated at government expense, something that is unprecedented in the BOP. Mrs. Trentadue declined the offer and informed Acting Warden Carter that her son Jesse was a lawyer and he would contact her.

When Jesse finally reached Acting Warden Carter he had to argue with her and insist that an autopsy be performed. That too was mighty peculiar because the Federal Bureau of Prisons, which is part of the Justice Department, mandates an autopsy be conducted on any inmate who dies unexpectedly while in BOP custody.

It has never been explained why Kenney Trentadue, a federal prison inmate who had committed federal crimes in California, had been

Deadly Secrets

incarcerated only in federal prisons in California, who was on parole and reporting to a parole officer in Southern California, was then transferred halfway across the country for a parole revocation hearing. What is clear is that on August 21, 1995, while Kenneth Michael Trentadue was in the custody of agents employed by the U.S. government in Oklahoma City, his lifeless, bloody, battered and tortured body was released to employees from the Oklahoma State Medical Examiner's office. However, investigators from that office were not allowed to access the cell where Kenney is alleged to have committed suicide. It would be months before they would be allowed into that cell, and only after it had been cleaned and repainted.

Being at the FTC put Kenney Trentadue in close proximity to Timothy McVeigh, who was then being held at the federal prison in El Reno, Oklahoma. Kenney's death occurred only 11 days after the federal grand jury had issued its indictment against McVeigh, Nichols and Others Unknown.

By this time there were any number of people in Oklahoma City and elsewhere who didn't buy into the government's theory of the bombing, or the easy solution and tidy closure of the case with the arrests of the two men who were locked up some 30 miles away. No one could forget the man identified by federal investigators only as John Doe No. 2. Law enforcement officers nationwide had been searching furiously for this unidentified individual who was believed to be one of McVeigh's accomplices. The composite sketch of John Doe No. 2 had been circulated worldwide. The sketch was made from a witness's description of a man seen with McVeigh – who looked nothing like Terry Nichols. McVeigh himself was identified as John Doe No. 1.

The police description of John Doe No. 2 was of a man approximately 5'9", muscular, with dark hair and a tattoo of a dragon on his left forearm; he was driving an older model pickup truck.

As Jesse Trentadue began investigating his brother's death, he had no idea of the physical resemblance between Kenney and the man known only as John Doe No. 2. It would be years before the significance would become obvious.

Five days after Kenney's death, his battered and bruised body was received by a mortuary in Westminster, California. His mother Wilma, wife Carmen and sister Donna Sweeney were there to receive him.

The body was covered with a thick coat of mortician's makeup, but it couldn't hide the numerous injuries, including a gash across Kenney's throat, and bruises on his face and forehead. The women undressed the body and washed away the makeup. It was then that the horrible injuries to Kenney's body were visible. They photographed the body as evidence of the torture Kenney had endured prior to his death.

On August 30, Jesse flew to Dallas, where he hand-delivered a letter to the regional director of the BOP. That office oversees the Federal Transfer Center in Oklahoma City. He also sent copies of his letter to numerous Justice Department officials. The letter read in part: "I have enclosed as Exhibit A a photograph of Kenneth's body at the funeral . . . This is how you returned my brother to us . . . My brother had been so badly beaten that I personally saw several mourners leave the viewing to vomit in the parking lot! Anyone seeing my brother's body with his bruised and lacerated forehead, throat cut, and blue-black knuckles would not have concluded that his death was either easy or a 'suicide'!" Jesse concluded his letter as follows: "Had my brother been less of a man, your guards would have been able to kill him without inflicting so much injury to his body. Had that occurred, Kenney's family would be forever guilt-ridden with the pain of thinking that Kenneth took his own life and that we had somehow failed him. By making the fight he did for his life, Ken has saved us that pain and God bless him for that."

Jesse told me that: "David, Kenney took a whole lot of killin'. Those bastards had a fight on their hands. Kenney gave 'em more than they bargained for. I want every one of them to own up to what they did. We don't want their money. We just want the truth. They might not know it, but I'm one pissed-off hillbilly, and I'm gonna find out who killed my brother and why they did it. I'll never stop fighting for Kenney as long as I'm alive."

On September 1, 1995, BOP officials issued a press release announcing that Kenney's death had been ruled a suicide and that the injuries to his body were self-inflicted during his persistent attempts to cause himself serious injury or death. They later attempted to explain away the injuries with an elaborate scenario. Unfortunately for prison officials, that scenario is belied by logic and physical evidence at the scene of the crime.

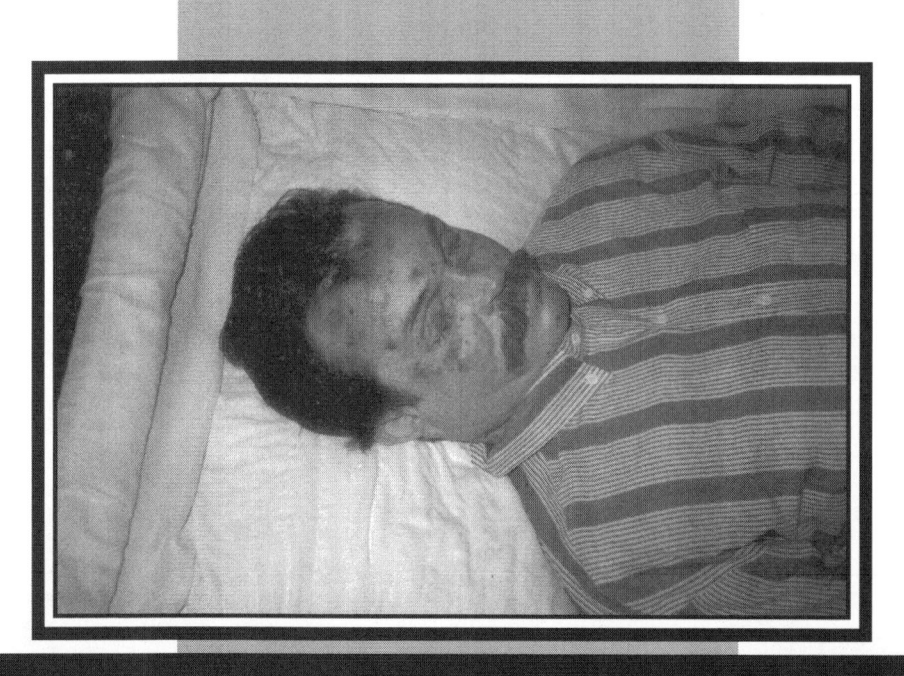

Kenneth Trentadue

The government contends that Trentadue's "extensive injuries, deposits of blood and, ultimately, hanging and death occurred in quite a short period of time, from approximately 2:38 a.m., at the earliest, to about 3:02 a.m., a space of approximately 24 minutes." There was no blood on the floor of Kenney's cell (709-A) at 2:38 a.m. Nothing was amiss.

The Oklahoma State Medical Examiner, Dr. Fred B. Jordan, who is known as a first-rate forensic pathologist, and who also went on to become a president of the National Association of Medical Examiners, testified that in 37 years of practice he had never seen a hanging with so much trauma. It took over three years before Dr. Jordan would eventually rule Kenney's death a suicide, and not until he had been the victim of, as he described it, "Mississippi Burning-style meddling and intimidation." Quoted in a 2006 Salt Lake City newspaper, Dr. Jordan called the local FBI "a bunch of toughs." He added that the Justice Department harassed and pressured him into signing off on the suicide theory. Dr. Jordon felt so threatened by the Justice Department and FBI that he requested a "protective audit" from the IRS because the "friggen FBI . . . might want to frame me in one way or another." Dr. Jordan took to traveling with a gun.

An expert hired by the government, nationally recognized pathologist Dr. John Smialek, described Kenney's death as "weird, because of the extensive trauma and massive blood loss." Weird would also explain the government's feeble explanations for Kenney's injuries.

The government claims that after guards at the FTC last saw Kenney alive in bed at 2:38 a.m., he used a pencil to write a suicide note on the wall of his cell, but did not sign his own name. Next, he supposedly patiently tore a bed sheet into dozens of strips. He then constructed a ligature from those strips. Once that was completed, Kenney remade his bed, climbed the wall of his cell and wove the bed-sheet rope into a metal vent above his sink. He then tried to hang himself, and was momentarily successful, but the rope broke. Kenny fell, hitting his buttocks on the edge of the sink, but doing no injury to them. The impact of his body on the sink caused him to ricochet across the cell headfirst into the corner of a metal desk at the end of his bunk, producing a major wound on his forehead.

The government says that the force of that impact caused Kenney to rotate 180 degrees and careen across his cell to smash his head into the wall, creating a second major wound on the right side of his head, leaving blood and hair on the wall of his cell and tearing extensive areas of skin off of his back. Despite striking the desk with such force, the impact did not disturb the coffee cup or any of the papers on the desk.

The government next claims that while unconscious from his two head wounds, Kenney rolled over on his stomach and bled profusely, depositing large pools of blood on the floor of his cell. When Kenney regained consciousness, he attempted to get up, but struck the back of his head on the metal stool attached to the desk, causing a third major wound on the back of his head. This third blow to his head further dazed Kenney, who then crawled on all fours with his clothing smearing blood on the floor. The government has never attempted to explain the various injuries to Kenny's knuckles and legs, or the fingerprint impressions on his arms.

The government states that Kenney finally got to his feet and staggered around, leaving blood deposits on the walls of his cell. He then stumbled to his bed and lay down to regain his senses. After a while, Kenney used two plastic toothpaste tubes or a plastic knife to cut his throat, leaving no blood on his pillowcase, sheet and blanket. When that second suicide attempt failed, Kenney reconstructed the bed-sheet rope and successfully hanged himself.

It is undisputed that Kenney's fingerprints were found on nothing in his cell but his personal papers. No sheet fibers or threads were found on his body or in his cell. It is also undisputed that Kenney's clothing is missing! The government contends that before his final suicide attempt, he took a washcloth and wiped his fingerprints from the pencil supposedly used to write the suicide note, from the plastic knife and/or toothpaste tubes he used to slash his throat and from every other item in the cell, except his personal papers. Kenney also carefully cleaned himself and his cell to remove all threads or fibers from the sheets torn to fashion the ligature. He then undressed and hid his bloodstained clothing (inside of a locked solitary confinement cell) so well that it has never been found.

It is undisputed that sound is amplified within the cells and housing units at the FTC. The government says that Kenney accomplished all of his injuries in absolute silence so as not to alert any nearby inmates or guards, and that he accomplished all of this within 17 minutes, in order to have been hanging more than six minutes, which rendered him dead and not able to be revived, when discovered at 3:03 a.m.

Eric Ellis, Dennis Williams, Kimberly Heath and Wiley Creasey were the guards on duty in the Special Housing Unit at the time of Kenney's death. They all swear that Kenney was alone and that no one entered his cell. These guards also swear they found Kenney hanging and eventually cut him down. The guards said the ligature, which Kenney allegedly used to hang himself with, consisted of two segments: the bed-sheet rope tied to the vent in his cell, which remained after he was purportedly cut down, and the knotted 23-inch bed-sheet noose that was around Kenney's neck after he was cut down.

Ellis, the guard who claims to have cut Kenney down, said that he cut the noose three to four inches above Kenney's head and left it around his neck. Tammy Corwine (formerly Tammy Gillis) was a field investigator for the Oklahoma State Medical Examiner when she came to the FTC on the morning of August 21, 1995, to retrieve Kenney's body. She spoke to the guards, who told her that it was physician assistant Carlos Mier who had cut Kenney down, not them. Corwine then asked Mier who had cut Kenney down, and he said it was the guards.

The official story of Kenney's death just didn't ring true with his brother. Jesse Trentadue vowed to learn the truth. His long investigation has taken him to places he could never have imagined, eventually leading him to discover a link to the Oklahoma City Bombing. Jesse eventually reached a shocking conclusion: that FBI agents tortured and killed his brother during a prison interrogation, apparently in the mistaken belief that Kenneth Trentadue was John Doe No. 2 – McVeigh's unidentified accomplice who got away.

If Jesse is right, and federal government employees killed his brother, they didn't realize what they had done by spilling Trentadue blood. Jesse has made it his life's mission to show them.

But that has proved to be a long, strange trip – not only Jesse's journey into the sprawling, twisted bombing conspiracy and its various alleged players, but also the possible serial murder case Jesse would soon uncover as he began digging into the mystery of his brother's death.

Astonishingly, Kenney wasn't the only dead prisoner. Soon Jesse discovered two more whose deaths were carbon copies of Kenney's. Who could possibly have killed these men – all three in federal custody, all in solitary confinement, all locked inside cells to which only federal correctional officers had keys?

Who might seem obvious.

But why?

10

CHAPTER TEN

COVER-UP

The concealment of the circumstances of Kenneth Trentadue's death, which began immediately, would eventually lead all the way to the upper echelons of the Justice Department, and continues to this day. Why would such a massive cover-up be undertaken to protect some rogue prison guards who went over the top with an inmate? As Jesse Trentadue would discover, something much deeper was going on here.

The initial autopsy report issued by Dr. Fred B. Jordan, who, at the time was the chief medical examiner for the State of Oklahoma, details the serious injuries that Kenney suffered prior to his death. Dr. Jordan listed the cause of death as "traumatic asphyxia" and the manner of death as "unknown." Dr. Jordan is the same medical examiner whose staff faced the grim task of identifying the victims from the Oklahoma City Bombing. His reputation has consistently been above reproach, and he was hailed as a prosecution witness in the trials of McVeigh and Nichols.

From the onset of the Trentadue investigation, Dr. Jordan's staff faced one obstacle after another. The hindrance came from federal employees at all levels. On the morning of August 21, 1995, after the discovery of Kenney's body, Investigator Corwine, from Dr. Jordan's office, was not allowed into cell 709-A of the Federal Transfer Center, where Kenney was alleged to have committed suicide. She was only allowed to peer into the cell through a small window on the door. A few hours later, Chief Investigator Kevin Rowland from Dr. Jordan's office telephoned the FTC and informed Acting Warden Carter that Kenney's death looked like a homicide. Rowland repeatedly asked the acting warden to call in the FBI to investigate the death and to immediately secure the crime scene. When Carter refused, Rowland informed her that he was going to contact the FBI himself. He placed that call at 8:10 a.m. on August 21.

Lt. Kenneth W. Freeman, the prison's special investigative agent, conducted the Federal Bureau of Prisons' investigation at the FTC. Records obtained by Jesse Trentadue reveal that Lt. Freeman's investigation was fraught with errors, lies, and was an intentional cover-up. Those actions began almost immediately. Pursuant to Oklahoma State statutes, the State of Oklahoma had concurrent jurisdiction with the Federal Government over the FTC. The Oklahoma State Medical Examiner was supposed to have control over the death scene, which could not be disturbed, cleaned or destroyed without his approval. BOP policy required that Kenney's alleged suicide be investigated by a panel of psychologists from other BOP institutions; that a detailed report of the motives and methods of his alleged suicide, known as a psychological reconstruction, be prepared; and that FTC personnel "Shall handle the site with the same level of protection as any crime scene in which death has occurred to insure that available evidence and documentation is preserved to provide data and support for subsequent investigators doing a psychological reconstruction."

Before 8:00 a.m., on August 21, officials at BOP Headquarters notified the prison administration at FTC-Oklahoma City that a psychological reconstruction team was on its way to the FTC to investigate. The FTC administration knew that the team would be arriving at the institution that very afternoon. Nevertheless, Kenney's cell was hurriedly cleaned and "sanitized" beforehand. To date, Kenney's is the only so-called suicide within the Federal Bureau of Prisons for which a psychological reconstruction was not conducted.

FTC inmates Steve Cole, George Orellana and Antoine Gist cleaned Trentadue's cell. They were instructed to scrub down the crime scene, and FTC employees Rosonda Chisholm and Keri Nelson supervised them. The job of sanitizing the cell was completed by 1:50 p.m. on the afternoon of August 21. By intentionally disregarding the specific instructions of the medical examiner's staff, the employees at FTC destroyed crucial physical evidence such as blood splatter. Nelson stated there was blood within four feet of the floor. Located just inside the cell door was a distress button for alerting staff to emergencies within the cell, thereby summoning help. Nelson, Cole, Orellana and Gist later testified there was a bloody handprint near, but not on, the button and that the handprint streaked down the wall, as though a person was collapsing trying to reach the distress alarm. The presence of the handprint was later confirmed through a Luminol test, which allows investigators to detect blood not visible to the naked eye. Prior to the cleanup, Freeman failed to photograph the bloody handprint during his investigation. He also failed to photograph the other blood splatter observed by the inmates and staff in Kenney's cell.

It was Freeman's duty to conduct the initial investigation, including preserving evidence. He had been trained in preservation of crime scenes, including the recognition of blood splatter and cast-off, which results during an assault. At approximately 8:30 a.m., on the morning of August 21, Freeman met with his superiors at the FTC. He left that meeting to telephone the Oklahoma City field office of the FBI. Freeman spoke with FBI Special Agent Jeffery Jenkins. Freeman informed Agent Jenkins that Kenney had committed suicide. Freeman did not tell Jenkins about the blood in the cell or the extensive injuries on the inmate's body. Freeman lied, informing the agent that the scene of the suicide had already been cleaned. Why? Freeman then told the agent he would complete his report of the suicide investigation and fax a copy to the FBI. Freeman admitted he never intended to do that investigative report, or to provide a copy to the FBI. He stated that if a guard told him an inmate committed suicide, there was no need for him to conduct an investigation. All he needed to do was "come up with some explanation as to how Kenney Trentadue got the head trauma."

Freeman later admitted to having lied to Jenkins and others in order to have the crime scene destroyed. He showed no remorse for his actions, stating: "If I have to take a hit for it, so be it." But Freeman certainly was not acting alone.

In the early morning hours of August 21, Freeman took a series of photographs of Trentadue and the cell where he died. The negatives of the 35mm photographs and one of two rolls of film mysteriously disappeared. That same morning, Operations Lieutenant Stuart A. Lee also took a series of Polaroid photographs, but they too mysteriously disappeared. It would be years later, and only after all of the official investigations into Kenneth Trentadue's death were concluded, before the missing photographs were discovered by the FBI in its files.

In order to somehow support the theory that Kenney committed suicide, a psychologist at FTC left a meeting with his supervisors about the Trentadue case to prepare a report stating that Trentadue had been placed on suicide watch shortly before his death. The psychologist, David Wedeking, later admitted under oath that the report was false and there had been no suicide watch.

Somehow, by August 22, within 24 hours of the discovery of Kenney Trentadue's body, the Justice Department's Office of the Inspector General completed its first investigation of the Trentadue case, concluding that no "prosecutable federal crime had occurred." On that same date, Kevin Rowland, the investigator from Dr. Jordan's office, filed a murder complaint with the Oklahoma City office of the FBI stating: "That the authorities at FTC's version of victim's (Trentadue) alleged suicide is not consisted with Medical Examiner's report."

Two days later, BOP Director Kathleen Hawk-Sawyer formed a board of inquiry to investigate Kenney's death and the circumstances surrounding it. In a very strange and surprising move, she appointed BOP attorney Michael D. Hood to head the investigation. She instructed Hood to treat all reports prepared by the inquiry team as "attorney work product." This designation meant that the Justice Department investigation was being conducted to defend against any civil litigation brought by the Trentadue family. More importantly, this action was being undertaken by the BOP at the direction of Director Hawk-Sawyer even before the Trentadue family had received Kenney's body. The Hood-led investigation included a week spent at FTC-Oklahoma City "preserving evidence," including the photographs that disappeared until years later.

On October 12, 1995, Assistant Director and BOP General Counsel Wallace H. Chaney contacted the BOP's Office of Internal Affairs, which was also investigating Kenney's death. The purpose of Chaney's e-mail was to warn internal affairs investigators that "there is a great likelihood of a lawsuit by the family of the inmate." In lawyer speak, Chaney was instructing the Office of Internal Affairs to be very careful about any findings it made with respect to the conduct of Justice Department employees in the manner of Kenney's death, since those findings could later be used as evidence against the Justice Department.

On November 16, 1995, BOP attorney Ann Tran met with FBI Agent Jenkins to discuss the Trentadue case, the investigation and what jurisdiction the Oklahoma State Medical Examiner's Office had over that investigation. Attorney Tran informed Jenkins that because the FTC was not on federal ground, the Justice Department was "obliged to follow state law," and therefore, "the Medical Examiner is entitled to all information and records pertaining to the deceased in doing their investigation." Jenkins' response to Tran was to say: "He doesn't care about Oklahoma law" . . . and that if the Medical Examiner is "conducting an investigation for Trentadue's brother, then he gets nothing." That same day, BOP Regional Director for the South Central Region, Charles Turnbo, reported this conversation to Director Hawk-Sawyer. After a delay of almost three months, on November 16, 1995, Oklahoma State Medical Examiner's Investigator Kevin Rowland was finally allowed to inspect Kenney's cell.

Cell 709-A was now supposed to be a secured crime scene, sealed with crime scene tape within the custody and control of the BOP. Investigator Rowland was escorted to Kenney's cell by several DOJ employees, including attorney Tran, Capt. Sheffer, Lt. Freeman and FBI Special Agent Jenkins. In the presence of the Justice Department employees, Rowland asked Jenkins to have the handwriting on the cell wall analyzed. The BOP investigators had concluded that a message scribbled on the cell wall that read, "my mind is no longer its friend, love familia," was a suicide note left behind by Kenney. Rowland returned to the FTC and to Cell 709-A on December 14, 1995. The cell was secured with crime scene tape, but the handwriting had been painted over. The FBI Crime Lab, left with only photographs to work from in order to analyze the writing, reported that "due to the lack of detail in the submitted photographs [it] is doubtful if this hand printing will ever be identified with hand printing of a known individual." Who destroyed the original evidence and why has never been determined, but the crime scene was under the control of the Justice Department and its employees within the BOP.

Other evidence that mysteriously disappeared included the clothing worn by Kenney at the time of his death. When his body was discovered he was wearing bloodstained khaki pants and a bloodstained T-shirt. The missing photographs would eventually verify this fact. When the body was turned over to the medical examiner at 7:00 a.m. Kenney was dressed in bloodstained boxer shorts. An FBI memorandum states that Agent Jenkins left the clothing in the trunk of his car until it was putrefied, and that "Jenkins took the smelly, bloody clothing out of his car and now had it in the FBI office." The clothing disappeared, and has never been seen since. Agent Jenkins denies this ever occurred.

FBI Special Agent Tom Linn provided testimony in the Trentadue case. He provided some revealing details. He stated that on the top bunk mattress two separate types of blood were discovered. One was determined to be Kenney's blood. The other was not identified, and the FBI did not attempt to identify the unknown blood sample. Additionally, Agent Linn testified that BOP Lt. Freeman had failed to photograph the blood splatter or bloody handprint, and that he failed to collect blood and hair just inside of Kenney's cell. According to Agent Linn, this evidence "disappeared."

The officers arriving at Cell 709-A on the morning of Trentadue's death claim he was hanging and the body was then cut down. There remains a dispute over who actually cut down the body. The noose, which they claim was cut from Kenney's neck, was turned over to the medical examiner's investigator when the body was retrieved. The noose was provided to an expert with the Oklahoma State Bureau of Investigation. Douglas J. Perkins, a fabric expert, analyzed the evidence and determined that it had not been cut. The only cut marks made on the ligature were those made by Lt. Freeman on the portion of the bedsheet rope that he claims was attached to the vent in the cell. There was no evidence that the noose had ever been around Kenney's neck, and it certainly had not been cut.

A videotape that BOP staff claim to have made of Kenney's cell and body never made its way into the evidence collected during the investigations. BOP guard Roger T. Groover stated he used a video camera to record the cell and Kenney's hanging body. He testified under oath to the grand jury and to the Justice Department's Office of the Inspector General that he videotaped these images, and that the video camera was functioning properly. However, he later admitted he never saw Kenney hanging and never videotaped any hanging body. The Justice Department claims the video camera malfunctioned, resulting in only a two or three-second videotape of no evidentiary importance. Norman I. Perle, a video forensic expert, retained by the OIG, later examined that videotape. Mr. Perle opined the videotape had been erased. The OIG then obtained a second opinion from another forensic video expert, Bruce Koenig, who happened to be a former FBI employee. He gave the opinion that the tape had not been erased, and that the video camera must therefore have malfunctioned.

The physician assistant on duty at the FTC at the time of Trentadue's death was Carlos A. Mier. He told federal investigators that he performed CPR on Kenney's body when he arrived at the cell. Mier even signed a sworn affidavit to this effect, detailing the resuscitative efforts he made. He provided similar testimony before the grand jury. Mier later admitted under oath he had lied about performing CPR. He also denied cutting Trentadue down from the vent in the cell and claimed Trentadue was on the floor when he arrived. BOP guard Eric Ellis told investigators that Kenney was "gurgling" when they reached his cell, but that the officer in charge that morning, Lt. Lee, refused to allow the cell door to be opened. Lee claimed he made the decision to wait before opening the cell door because he "knew for sure" that Kenney "was dead and thus not concerned with taking any immediate emergency action."

Some of the injuries to Kenney's body found by the medical examiner could not possibly have been self-inflicted. Dr. Jordan found a bruise on Kenney's anal verge, the portion of the body just above the anal opening where the buttocks come together, which did not involve any injury to the surrounding buttocks. Dr. Smialek testified that such injuries to the anal verge without injury to the buttocks only occur as a result of an assault. Forensic pathologist, Dr. Miles Jones, concurred, stating that this injury was most likely the result of Kenney being kicked.

Other injuries on Kenney's body that were obviously not self-inflicted were the fingertip bruises on his biceps. Dr. Smialek said these injuries were a result of Kenney having been "grabbed while alive." The bruises on the bottom of Kenney's right foot were also not self-inflicted. Such injuries are only produced by severe accidents or as the result of torture. Dr. Jones stated that bruises such as those on the bottom of Kenney's foot would not occur as a result of walking or jumping.

Dr. Jones stated that in his professional opinion Kenney's death was a homicide and that he died by strangulation. Dr. Jordan also testified that the ligature marks on Kenney's neck were consistent with strangulation or hanging. Dr. Jordan's decision to change the manner of death in the Trentadue case from "unknown" to suicide came almost three years later, and only after prolonged pressure from the federal government.

In a memorandum to the Trentadue case file (number 9504017), Dr. Jordan wrote in detail on December 20, 1995, of his frustrations with federal officials over the Trentadue case. That memorandum reads in part:

> At approximately 3:00 p.m., not having heard anything from the District of Columbia (United States Attorney Eric Holder) I called Assistant U.S. Attorney, in Oklahoma City, Mrs. Arlen Joplin. I indicated to her my frustration with the lack of communication with the [AG's office.] She led me to believe that they had in fact been called by an assistant U.S. Attorney who basically probably told them to deal with me. I advised her that I felt that the Trentadue problem was a very serious issue that needed the full support of the investigative services of the FBI. I believe I further informed her that last week in frustration I indicated to agent Hunt of the FBI that it could not help but occur to me that perhaps the FBI and the Bureau of Prisons were not expediting this investigation as quickly as we hoped would occur. I told her I thought there was a very serious problem at the prison and approximately at this time Mr. Ryan (United States Attorney in Oklahoma City) also got on the line. I indicated I felt that Mr. Trentadue had been abused

and tortured and at this point was not sure whether his death could be explained as a suicide, or whether it should be regarded as a homicide. At any event it certainly needs to be investigated as a homicide.

Dr. Jordan's suspicions regarding the FBI were right on target. In a December 6, 1995 communication, the FBI's Oklahoma City office reported to FBI Headquarters that Dr. Jordan was a "loose cannon" and that "the Medical Examiner's findings will probably rule that . . . [Trentadue's] death was a homicide." On that same day FBI Special Agent Jenkins reported to FBI Headquarters that "the new Warden at the FTC will not allow any of the guards/officials to take polygraph examinations. The prison guards are represented by a strong union which will probably also object to their members taking a polygraph."

The BOP had been pressuring the FBI as well. In a November 16, 1995 communication from BOP South Central Regional Director Charles Turnbo to BOP Director Hawk-Sawyer, he informed her "we're continuing to 'push' the FBI to conclude the investigation on the suicide. . ." DOJ employees were circling the wagons and stonewalling at every juncture.

Around this same time the first major news story about the Trentadue case appeared when *CNN* broadcast an eight-minute story on its national news. An article appeared in *The Spotlight* that same month. After reading about the case, I contacted Jesse Trentadue in early December 1995. I told him who I was and that in May of that year I had spent over a week in the Special Housing Unit at the FTC, where Kenney died, while I was in transit from Lompoc, California, to Allenwood, Pennsylvania. I told him something else: "Mr. Trentadue, I don't know what happened to your brother, but I know that he could not have committed suicide in his cell on the SCU at the FTC. Those cells are suicide proof. There's no way to reach the vent, which is at the top of a 12-foot ceiling, and even if you could reach it, the air holes are tiny and there would be no way to tie anything through them."

This was the beginning of my long association with Jesse. Over the years, he and I stayed in touch and have developed a friendship as we both searched for the truth regarding Kenney's death.

During the time when federal officials and others were actively involved in obstructing justice in the Trentadue case, federal prosecutors were preparing their case against Timothy McVeigh and Terry Nichols. Dr. Jordan was a crucial government witness in the Oklahoma City Bombing case, and his refusal to sign off on suicide as the manner of death in the Trentadue case was an ongoing source of friction with some law enforcement officials.

In late 1995, Dr. Jordan made a visit to the FTC to personally inspect the cell where Kenney died. During that inspection and while he was at the prison, guards threatened him. The threats were so serious that Dr. Jordan reported them to the FBI, but nothing was ever done about the matter.

In February 1996, Oklahoma City Homicide Detective Tom Bevel reviewed some of the evidence in the Trentadue case. He was not shown the original photographs, but rather third-generation copies, as the negatives and one roll of film were missing at that time. He also was not shown the Groover videotape or the Polaroid photographs taken by Lt. Lee. From the limited evidence, however, Bevel concluded that based upon the blood-flow pattern on the body, Kenney had been wearing clothing at the time of his death. Bevel recommended to the FBI that "the inmate's clothing should be examined to determine the type, location and distribution of any blood stains." Obviously, Bevel had not been told of the missing clothing.

On April 14, 1996, a BOP assistant director wrote to U.S. Senator Dianne Feinstein in an attempt to head off any inquiry by the Senate Judiciary Committee into the manner of Kenney's death. BOP Assistant Director Wallace Chaney assured Senator Feinstein that "a representative of the Oklahoma Medical Examiner's Office came to the institution, reviewed Kenneth Michael Trentadue, and examined the cell. The cell had not been disturbed except for the removal of the body." Chaney's representation to Feinstein was not true.

On July 6, 1996, a federal grand jury was convened to investigate Kenney's death. However, unlike most grand juries, this one was not conducted by the local U.S. Attorney's Office, but rather by attorneys Kevin Foster and Sheryl Robinson from Main Justice in Washington. Someone at the top wanted total control of the Trentadue investigation and the cover-up. This grand jury was nothing but a show that the

Justice Department orchestrated from start to finish. Witnesses perjured themselves, evidence was never presented, then turned up in FBI offices years later. One glaring question remains. Why?

On January 15, 1997, Dr. William Gormley of the Armed Forces Institute of Pathology completed his review of the autopsy of Kenney's body, which Dr. Gormley undertook at the request of Justice Department Civil Rights Division attorneys Kevin Foster and Sheryl Robinson. Dr. Gormley told the attorneys that because of the destruction of the crime scene, he agreed with the medical examiner's conclusion that the manner of Kenney's death should correctly be listed as "unknown." Dr. Gormley went on to say, however, he believed "the deceased was assaulted."

On January 28, 1997, then Deputy Attorney General Eric Holder presided over a highly unethical, if not illegal, meeting of the Justice Department's Civil Rights Division attorneys conducting the grand jury, and with Torts Branch attorneys who would later defend the Justice Department against a civil lawsuit brought by the Trentadue family. The subject of that meeting was "the Trentadue matter." The meeting took place long before the Trentadue family filed its lawsuit. The notes of the meeting are claimed to be privileged under the "work product doctrine," which means the purpose of the meeting was to defend a civil lawsuit, not to investigate Kenney's death.

On March 25, 1997, the Justice Department attorneys conducting the grand jury accused Jesse Trentadue of being on a "campaign to discredit the Federal Government." They held a meeting with certain FBI agents to discuss the possibility of indicting Jesse for "obstruction [of justice] or fraud. . ." The consensus of those present at the meeting was not to open a separate investigation of Jesse Trentadue, because he would have to be notified of the investigation and that he was a target. The Justice Department attorneys and the FBI agreed to secretly investigate Jesse under the guise of investigating Kenney's death. The Justice Department recruited a known FBI informant who was incarcerated within the BOP to assist them. BOP inmate James Hauser agreed to place a "yoke of silence" around Jesse Trentadue's neck by testifying that Jesse had paid inmates to perjure themselves. Hauser was polygraphed, failed the polygraph, but was nevertheless presented to the grand jury to give perjured testimony.

On April 11, 1997, *NBC Dateline* aired a show on Kenney Trentadue's death, including interviews with Senator Orrin G. Hatch and Dr. Jordan, the medical examiner. Hatch described the Justice Department's handling of the Trentadue case as "colossal incompetence." The Senator went on to say that the "possibility of cover-up" is "certainly something you can't ignore." In the strongest language, the Senator said: "There are a lot of things that just are phony about this, that just don't add up . . . There is no excuse for anybody covering this up. Now let me tell you something. This case isn't going to go away. Congress isn't going to go away. We want answers. We want to know what happened."

Dr. Jordan was equally powerful in his comments on *NBC Dateline*. When asked if he had ever seen a suicide like, this Jordan responded: "No. Not only have I not seen it in 20, almost 20 years of forensic practice . . . and I presented this informally to colleagues from other states and I have not encountered one who had ever seen anything like this before in a . . .in a suicide." More importantly, Jordan was asked whether some of the trauma to Kenney's body, such as the bruising on the underside of his arms, was self-inflicted. Dr. Jordan answered: "No, I think that was done by someone else." Following the *Dateline* program, Dr. Jordan wrote a memorandum to the Trentadue case file stating: "The Dateline program on 11/8 Apr. 97 was completely accurate. . ."

Within several weeks of the *Dateline* broadcast, Senator Hatch had an opportunity to question then Attorney General Janet Reno about the Trentadue case during a Judiciary Committee hearing. Hatch informed Reno that: "It is apparent to me that not only are the facts suspicious, it looks like someone in the Bureau of Prisons or someone having relations with the Bureau of Prisons has murdered this man."

The Justice Department attorneys conducting the grand jury contacted Dr. Gormley again on May 29, 1997. They asked him to come and testify before the grand jury in June. They wanted Dr. Gormley to testify that "it might be possible these [Kenney's] injuries are self-inflicted." Dr. Gormley refused and immediately notified the Oklahoma Medical Examiner's Office of this occurrence. Dr. Gormley told those he spoke with that he was now even more convinced "that this man was murdered."

In response to a Freedom of Information request for information about Kenney's death made by Jesse Trentadue to the FBI, he was informed on June 27, 1997, that his request was being denied because of the ongoing investigation into the circumstances of his brother's death. The FBI intentionally misled Jesse when it stated: "Please be advised that you are not the target of this investigation."

Four days later Dr. Jordan spoke again with an Assistant U.S. Attorney for the Western District of Oklahoma, which includes Oklahoma City. Dr. Jordan told the Assistant U.S. Attorney in a memo that the "federal Grand Jury [investigating the Trentadue case] is a part of a cover-up," and that he "feel[s] it is likely that this man was killed." Despite BOP employees being the target of the grand jury, the Assistant U.S. Attorney immediately conveyed Jordan's comments to the BOP.

On July 3, 1997, Dr. Jordan went on national television and stated that Kenneth Trentadue was "very likely murdered," but because of the destruction of the crime scene, "I am unable to prove it." He further stated that the Justice Department's destruction of evidence in the case was incompetent, or worse, "planned."

The grand jury investigation concluded on August 13, 1997, with a no bill of indictment. Those results were then kept secret while the Justice Department put into place a "roll-out plan," which it termed the "Trentadue mission."

The paper trail on the roll-out plan is scant. However, e-mails and handwritten notes by those working under Deputy Attorney General Holder in the Justice Department have surfaced. These documents paint a clear picture of a wide-ranging and cynical scheme, run directly by Holder, to quash the Trentadue family's efforts to have Kenney's homicide investigated, and to deflect congressional oversight and media attention from the shocking circumstances of his death.

Holder chaired meetings at which the roll-out plan was developed. Those responsible for implementing the plan saw their task as applying major spin treatment to Senator "Hatch and possibly Dorgan," according to Justice Department emails, to dissuade the Senators from further questioning the circumstances of Kenney's death, and to "reach out to the press before or at the same time that we expect Trentadue to do so."

The continuing efforts to prepare for the announcement of the no bill of indictment included a memorandum authored by Kathleen Timmons, chief of the FBI's Color of Law Unit. On October 5, 1997,

Timmons wrote to her superiors within the FBI advising them that "efforts had been underway at DOJ to advise Senator Orrin Hatch of the press release before it is publicly announced." Timmons also reported to FBI Director Louis Freeh and others that she had viewed the "non-existent" Groover videotape, and that as a result of viewing that tape: "There is a potential perjury issue regarding a Bureau of Prisons paramedic who indicated he administered CPR to the deceased Trentadue and the evidence of a videotape does not indicate CPR was administered. Other serious issues are involved in the case regarding BOP personnel's mishandling of the corpse and the potential crime scene and the aftermath of Trentadue's death."

Timmons later wrote her FBI superiors expressing her view that because of the lack of efforts to resuscitate the victim, Carlos Mier might face state criminal charges.

On October 9, 1997, the Justice Department issued its press release announcing the conclusion of the grand jury, and the decision not to issue any indictment. The press release made no mention of the grand jury having secretly concluded two months earlier.

The evening of the press release, as part of the roll-out plan, Deputy Attorney General Holder met with Senator Hatch. The stated purpose of the meeting was to defuse Judiciary Committee oversight and media inquiry into Kenney's death. In fact, one e-mail by a Holder staffer stated that: "we ain't looking for press on this. Hill takes priority." The meeting apparently didn't go exactly as planned by Holder, however, because the next day, Senator Hatch issued a press release stating in part that he intended to "hold an oversight hearing later this year to examine the facts surrounding the death of Mr. Trentadue and the Department's handling of the matter to date."

Hatch also gave an exclusive interview later that day to *Fox News* in which he spoke out against the results of the grand jury and the Justice Department's handling of the case:

> I met with the Deputy Attorney General just last night on this. . . All of this is very, very upsetting to a lot of people, including myself. Now, we haven't had a hearing on this lately because of the ongoing federal investigation. But now that the federal people have completed their analysis of this and their investigation,

> I think we will hold a hearing between now and the end of the year and just see what we can do to get to the bottom of this. . .There is a lot wrong with this case and I hope somebody will get to the bottom of it. But apparently the federal government hasn't been able to do so. . .Yep, it has the aroma of cover-up . . . And like I say, it does look bad. Somebody has not told the truth here and somebody is, in my opinion, covering up.

These are the words of Senator Hatch, his direct quote from the *Fox News* interview. Hatch was then the chairman of the Senate Judiciary Committee, with the authority to convene the hearing he spoke of. Unfortunately, that hearing never happened. It did not take place because, following Senator Hatch's public announcement, at the apparent urging of Assistant Attorney General Holder, a delegation from the FBI approached Oklahoma Senator Don Nickles to ask for his assurances that there would be no Senate investigation.

There were two such meetings between Senator Nickles and FBI representatives. The first was on December 4, 1997, and the second was on January 23, 1998. Records relating to these meetings were made public as a part of the Trentadue family's wrongful death civil lawsuit against the Justice Department. Those records reveal that FBI Headquarters and the Justice Department had approved both meetings.

The first meeting lasted one hour and 45 minutes. Senator Nickles was not even a member of the Senate Judiciary Committee. Yet, he is reported to have promised the FBI delegation "that it would be his decision whether a Senate inquiry into this matter would be conducted . . .[and] he was not inclined to initiate such a review." At the conclusion of the second meeting with Senator Nickles, on January 23, 1998, the Senator is reported to have thanked the agents for their time and candidness regarding his questions. The FBI report dated January 28, 1998, concluded with the following: "He also intimated that he had a significant role in determining whether this matter would require Congressional review, and that such action would most likely not be necessary." The FBI officials who met with Senator Nickles included the Special Agent in Charge of the FBI Oklahoma City Division, Thomas M. Kuker, Supervisory Special Agent John P. Mabry, Special Agent Tom Linn and CDC Henry C. Gibbons. The first meeting occurred in Senator Nickles' Tulsa office and the second at his Oklahoma City office. Prior approval for the meetings was provided by Inspector in Charge John E. Collingwood at FBI Headquarters in Washington, D.C.

During the time period from October 9, 1997 through January 1998, both Dr. Jordan and Senate Judiciary Chairman Orrin Hatch continued to speak out publicly about the very flawed investigation and grand jury decision in the Trentadue case. Following the Justice Department's press release on October 9, 1997, Dr. Jordan issued his own press release in which he said that he personally found the results of the grand jury "disappointing, but not surprising in view of the circumstances." The medical examiner went on to say: "From the outset, the Federal Government through its refusal to cooperate in allowing a thorough technical scene investigation by competent police technical investigation unit assured that adequate scientific answers to how Mr. Trentadue received his myriad of injuries will never be available. The refusal further assured that we will never be able to prove to a reasonable certainty if Mr. Trentadue hanged himself or if another asphyxial mechanism came into play. Since scientific investigation is the hallmark of good death investigation in our country, one has to wonder why the Government of the United States took the action that it did in this death investigation."

Twelve days later Dr. Jordan spoke by telephone with Senator Byron L. Dorgan, Democrat from North Dakota, about the Trentadue case. Dr. Jordan explained to Senator Dorgan that it was his feeling "that the investigation was crippled, the decedent was at least beaten, we haven't found the truth and probably won't." Dr. Jordan then went on to tell the Senator about his "lack of trust in the federal government. . . and the Department of Justice in particular."

On January 17, 1998, *Fox News* broadcast a story on Trentadue's death, and Senator Hatch was interviewed for that program. He again stated that he was "disappointed in the grand jury result," and because this case has the "aroma of cover-up." Hatch promised Judiciary Committee hearings. Hatch went further by telling *Fox News* that "somebody other than Trentadue beat Trentadue up."

By March 12, 1998, the Justice Department's harassment and threats to the Oklahoma State Medical Examiner and his staff had reached a boiling point. The Oklahoma Attorney General's Office intervened. In a letter written on this date by Assistant Attorney General Patrick Crawley to Justice Department attorneys, he stated:

> In the investigation into the death of Kenneth Trentadue, all the rules seem to have been set aside. In a sort of 'Alice Through the Looking Glass' set of circumstances, the truth has been obfuscated by the agendas of various federal agencies (mostly your clients) . . .In the process, your clients prevented the Medical Examiner from conducting a thorough and complete investigation into the death, destroyed evidence, and otherwise harassed and harangued Dr. Jordan and his staff. The absurdity of this situation is that your clients outwardly represent law enforcement or at least some arm of licit government. . .The real tragedy in this case appears to be the perversion of law through chicanery and the misuse of public trust under the guise of some aberrant form of federalism. In the succession of either illegal, negligent or just plan stupid acts, your clients succeeded in derailing the Medical Examiner's examination and, thereby, may have obstructed justice in this case. . . It appears that your clients and perhaps others within the Department of Justice, have been abusing the powers of their respective offices. If this is true, all Americans should be very frightened of your clients and the DOJ.

In late 1999, the final federal investigation of Kenney's death concluded, this one by the Justice Department's Office of the Inspector General. According to its report, dated November 18, 1999, the OIG found "no credible evidence that BOP or FBI officials conspired to cover-up the circumstances surrounding [Trentadue's] death." The OIG did recommend prosecution of three BOP employees and one FBI agent for allegedly committing perjury. It later became clear, however, from internal documents that the OIG knew these prosecutions would never happen. In advance of its report, an OIG official even consulted with a Justice Department attorney to find just the right language to include in the report – "lack of prosecutorial merit" – to signal that the Justice Department would not prosecute anyone.

After the report was issued, it was discovered that that former Oklahoma City Homicide Detective Tom Bevel, who had been hired by the Justice Department as an expert witness in its defense against the Trentadue family's lawsuit, actually helped write the OIG report.

Four years after the death of Kenney Trentadue, despite an uproar among an impressive list of concerned parties, the various state and federal investigations were over as of 1999. Investigators had singled out various federal employees, but astonishingly, no criminal charges would be filed against anyone for any crime.

But for Jesse Trentadue, the investigation was far from over. In fact, the mystery was about to get deeper. Dead prisoner No. 2 would soon surface, opening Jesse's continuing probe of Kenney's death into a potential serial murder investigation.

In late 1999, Jesse was preparing for trial in his family's wrongful death lawsuit against the Justice Department. Within a month of the OIG report being issued, Jesse had received a telephone call from one of his potential witnesses, BOP inmate Alden Gillis Baker, who was being held in the Special Housing Unit at the federal prison in Lompoc, California. Baker was a violent psychopath and the only witness to come forward and testify about Kenney's murder. Baker had provided a sworn deposition in the wrongful death suit Jesse was preparing.

BOP records reflect that Kenney Trentadue was placed in the same cell with Baker, who, because of his violence and psychological problems, was to be celled alone. The Justice Department claims Baker and Trentadue never occupied the same cell and that Baker was in fact celled in another part of the institution at the time of Kenney's death. But all permanent records that would show Baker's exact location within the Federal Transfer Center at the time of Kenney's death have disappeared. These records disappeared from widely dispersed locations, but before they vanished they were apparently in the possession of the FBI, because an FBI memorandum states that "records indicate that Baker and Trentadue occupied cell A709 on 8/20/95 and 8/21/95."

In his deposition, Baker said he and Kenney were in separate cells, but he witnessed part of the incident. Baker said he saw three BOP officers in full riot gear go into Kenney's cell, and heard sounds of a violent struggle. Baker said he saw the guards leaving the cell, and they were covered with blood. Afterwards, Baker said he heard "moaning" coming from Kenney's cell.

Baker had placed the telephone call to Jesse on December 9, 1999, to seek Jesse's help because Baker was being threatened by guards at USP-Lompoc. During that conversation, Baker told Jesse that he had placed a telephone call to Justice Department attorney Peter Schlossman, one of the lawyers representing the government in the Trentadue family's lawsuit. Baker told Schlossman about the threats he was receiving from BOP guards and asked for help. After hearing this, according to Baker, attorney Schlossman asked Baker if he was willing to say that his deposition testimony about having witnessed Kenneth Trentadue's murder was a lie. In response to the question, Baker told Schlossman that his deposition was the truth. Upon hearing this, Baker said Schlossman responded: "I have nothing further to say to you" and hung up the telephone.

On August 8, 2000, Alden Baker was found hanging by a bedsheet rope in his Special Housing Unit cell at USP-Lompoc. The Justice Department contends that Baker's death was a suicide, but it has refused to release any documents or evidence on the matter. The two telephone calls made by Baker where he spoke about the threats made against him were recorded by the BOP. The Justice Department refused to turn that recording over to the Trentadue family. Not only does Baker's death mirror Kenney Trentadue's, but it is exactly what another former FTC inmate, Nick Arcabasso, says he was told would happen to him if he continued to speak out about having heard FTC guard Rodney DeChamplain admit that "he killed Trentadue." Arcabasso said he was told he would "just be found swinging from a bed sheet."

Prior to the time of Baker's death, Jesse Trentadue had filed a motion for a protective order, to insure that Baker not be harmed. That motion was pending at the time of Baker's death. The circumstances certainly captured Jesse's attention. The death was a carbon copy of Kenney's, and it silenced a witness who might have been extremely compelling. Jesse had no way of knowing it at the time, but Alden Baker was only the second of three dead prisoners in Jesse Trentadue's path. The third was the one who might hold the key to solving the whole mystery of

Kenneth's death. But that discovery was still several years down the road.

On May 1, 2001, the Trentadue family's lawsuit was decided by the Honorable Timothy Leonard, a federal judge with the U. S. District Court for the Western District of Oklahoma. The judge ruled in favor of the Trentadues and entered a $1.1 million judgment against the Justice Department. The judgment was for the intentional infliction of emotional distress upon Kenneth Trentadue's family by the Justice Department. Because of perjury and destruction of evidence, however, the court was unable to find Trentadue's death was a homicide. The court did issue a scathing criticism about several Justice Department employees who had testified at the trial. "The testimony of PA Mier, Lt. Freeman and BOP Guard Robert Garza raise serious questions as to their truthfulness and reveal a lack of respect for the solemnity of sworn proceedings," the judge wrote. "From the time of Trentadue's death up to and including the trial these witnesses seemed unable to comprehend the importance of a truthful answer."

The court's statement about these Justice Department employees is not surprising. The earlier determination by the OIG, which was ignored by Attorney General Reno and Deputy Attorney General Holder, had found that the Justice Department employees had lied to officials, destroyed or mishandled evidence, and obstructed justice. They were all given a get-out-of-jail-free card and protected from prosecution.

The Justice Department appealed the court's judgment twice. After prolonged appeals, the judgment was reduced to $1 million and paid to the Trentadue family in 2008. Jesse told me: "This was never about money. All we ever wanted was to know the truth about Kenney and for those bastards who killed him to be held accountable."

To learn the truth, there was more digging to do – a lot more.

11

CHAPTER ELEVEN

SEARCHING FOR JOHN DOE NO. 2

Early on in his investigation into Kenney's death, Jesse Trentadue received a telephone call that he paid scant attention to. The caller, who didn't identify himself, said: "Look, your brother was murdered by the FBI. There was an interrogation that went wrong." The anonymous caller also said: "He fit a profile." There was a mention of bank robberies and bank robbers, but no real details. Jesse put the call out of his mind and pursued facts he could verify.

In January 2000, I passed on a message from Timothy McVeigh to Jesse Trentadue. I had been exchanging information with McVeigh for several months as a part of our bargain relating to my book. At recreation I'd shown McVeigh a series of photographs taken by the Trentadue family of Kenney's body, depicting his many injuries. McVeigh had mentioned the murder at the FTC previously, and I had informed him of my friendship with Jesse.

McVeigh was the first person to point out a possible connection between Kenney's murder and the possibility that Kenney was mistaken for John Doe No. 2, who McVeigh claimed was Richard Guthrie. McVeigh said: "The first time I saw a picture of Trentadue and learned of his death, I knew instantly that someone thought he was Richard

Guthrie and that them good 'ole boys in Oklahoma killed him because they thought he was involved in Oklahoma City."

If true, this could be the breakthrough Jesse needed. Considering the source, Jesse was interested but skeptical.

According to McVeigh, he had first learned about Kenney's murder through his correspondence with a reporter with the *Oklahoma Gazette* published in Oklahoma City. That reporter, Phil Bacharach, later published some of McVeigh's letters in the May 2001 issue of *Esquire* magazine. Bacharach had reported for the *Gazette* on the mysteries surrounding the Trentadue case.

I explained to Jesse what McVeigh had told me, and that Richard Guthrie was one of the bank robbers known as the Midwest Bank Bandits, and a member of the Aryan Republican Army. Jesse remembered the anonymous caller from years before, and the substance of that call. Could there be a connection between the Oklahoma City Bombing investigation and his brother's murder? The thought seemed preposterous at first, but nothing about Kenney's case had made any sense. Jesse had never understood why there had been such a massive cover-up by the federal government. Why would top-level officials go to such great lengths to hide the truth about one prisoner's death? Far-fetched as it seemed, if true, McVeigh's lead could provide the answer to all those questions.

The physical description of the Oklahoma City Bombing suspect known as John Doe No. 2, and widely disseminated by law enforcement, was of a muscular man, with dark complexion, 185 pounds and approximately 5'8" to 5'10" tall, possibly driving a brown pickup truck. An eyewitness stated that John Doe No. 2 had a very distinctive and unusual tattoo, possibly a serpent or a dragon.

Kenney Trentadue was 5'7" tall, weighed 175 pounds, had a sun-tanned complexion, full head of hair, mustache, and was "built like a bull and strong as an ox," according to Jesse. Most strikingly, the report on Kenney's arrest at the Mexican border includes mention of a distinctive dragon tattoo on Kenney's arm.

McVeigh's information looked more and more intriguing. Still, Jesse was pursuing multiple leads. He placed John Doe No. 2 in his large collection of clues, and waited for something more to materialize.

Three years later, in 2003, the phone call came. It was ace investigative reporter J.D. Cash, calling Jesse for the first time. The Trentadue case, Kenney's photographs and other information had been widely reported, not just in Oklahoma, but nationally. Cash knew the case. Also, though Jesse didn't know this, Cash and I had talked a few weeks earlier on the phone, and I had shared the information about the McVeigh tip on John Doe No. 2.

Cash was excited, a reporter chasing a hot story. He told Jesse he had been doing deep research on Richard Guthrie and the ARA. Cash had some questions about Kenney, and asked Jesse if he was sitting down.

Cash wanted to know about Kenney's tattoo. What type of vehicle was he driving when he was arrested at the border?

Cash and Jesse compared information, and Jesse soon understood just how closely Kenney resembled the co-leader of the Aryan Republican Army. Richard Lee Guthrie stood 5'7" tall, weighed 175 pounds and had a dark complexion. He had a stocky solid build, a full head of hair and a mustache.

But there was more. Kenney and Guthrie were both bank robbers. Without a doubt, Cash told Jesse, the FBI had immediately targeted ARA members as potential suspects in the bombing. All you had to do was read the newspaper to know this. Within days of the bombing, there were front-page articles in *The New York Times*, *The Kansas City Star* and *U.S. News and World Report*, about possible links between the ARA bank robberies, McVeigh and the bombing. Apprehending these fugitive unidentified bank robbers now became even more of a priority for the FBI.

As Cash learned, FBI agents and analysts now embarked on an ambitious mission: to identify all known bank robbers within the United States. A data bank was established to organize the information. All known facts relating to the BOMBROB case were entered into the system. That included terms used by the robbers, physical descriptions, weapons used, and escapes from the hold-up scenes. A computer program then compared those facts to known individuals previously convicted or suspected of committing bank robberies. Any cases that involved similar facts were flagged for further investigation. Cash learned that one name flagged was that of Kenneth Michael Trentadue, also known as Vance Paul Brockway.

Cash told Jesse that the FBI had Kenney's photograph, artists' renderings of the then-unidentified ARA bank robbery suspects, and, of course, the composite sketch of John Doe No. 2. Though Kenney Trentadue had no involvement in the bombing, he fit the FBI's profile perfectly, right down to the signature moves he made while committing his bank jobs.

During his bank robberies in the early 1980s, Kenney used a firearm and this language: "Get down, get down. This is a robbery, let's not make it a homicide." Little did the victims know that Kenney had disabled his weapon to ensure it couldn't actually be discharged. Guthrie and his crew used similar phrases, such as, "Get down, get down, no alarms, no hostages," during their bank heists. Other similarities included: no one being harmed during the robberies, only money from the tellers or within easy access being taken, and fast-paced robberies that took only a minute or two from start to finish. Some of the ARA robberies featured only one gunman inside of the bank, the same as with Kenney's crimes.

Jesse listened intently. Finally, after eight long years, he was connecting the dots. It was becoming deadly clear how Kenney Trentadue might have gotten swept up in the manhunt for possible accomplices of Timothy McVeigh. When Cash sent Jesse photographs of Richard Guthrie, Jesse laid one next to a photo of Kenney. They were look-alikes.

This stunning discovery would focus Jesse's investigation going forward. He now believed that Timothy McVeigh was right on target about Kenney being mistaken for John Doe No. 2. Before, Jesse had struggled in the dark, confronting one mystifying question after another as to the surprising behavior of the federal government in concealing the circumstances of Kenney's death.

Now, Jesse was beginning to fathom an extremely disturbing possibility: somewhere inside the government, some unknown players had been secretly involved in the Oklahoma City Bombing. Afterwards, those players apparently moved swiftly and ruthlessly to cover their tracks, so that Timothy McVeigh would be left shouldering responsibility as the lone mastermind.

2 Men Sought In Connection With The Oklahoma City Bombing

Described as being between 5-9 and 5-10.
Weighing between 175 and 180 lbs.
Visible tattoo below the sleeve of a tee-shirt.

Described as being between 5-10 and 5-11
Weighing between 180 and 185 lbs.

John Doe No. 1   John Doe No. 2

The first time I saw a picture of Trentadue and learned of his death, I knew instantly that someone thought he was Richard Guthrie and that them good ole boys in Oklahoma killed him because they thought he was involved in Oklahoma City.

— Timothy McVeigh

McVeigh's prison ID

One man, who knew too much, stood in the way. That was John Doe No. 2, an accomplice of McVeigh's – seen with him in the Ryder truck delivering the bomb. This man might have known enough to unravel the whole story of the bomb plot, and lead back to its prime movers. If Jesse could find the government insiders involved in the bombing, he knew he would have his brother's killers in his grasp.

But not so fast: Dead prisoner No. 3 had now surfaced as part of the mystery, complicating everything.

One glaring fact from J.D. Cash jumped out at Jesse. Richard Guthrie was dead by an alleged suicide. He was found hanging in a jail cell. Struck by the similarities between the supposed suicides of Kenney, Alden Baker, and now Guthrie, Jesse couldn't ignore the possibilities.

I still remember Jesse's words: "David, I don't believe in coincidences, and especially not when it comes to them sum' bitches involved with killin' Kenney!" Jesse was adamant in his conviction that something just didn't add up here.

I personally have looked into Guthrie's supposed suicide, which occurred on July 12, 1996, in the Kenton, Kentucky County Jail. Guthrie was awaiting disposition of the federal bank robbery cases against him. He was being held in an isolation cell in a special housing unit, away from other inmates and in protective custody. Records from the jail and from the U.S. Marshals Service relating to Guthrie and his suicide are surprisingly lacking in detail.

Apparently, if the records are to be believed, Guthrie was on a 20-minute watch by jail guards. He was confined to cell 973 alone on July 12. According to guards and the official jail logs, Guthrie was found hanging from a bed sheet in his cell at 6:06 a.m. by a deputy jailer doing a round. The official log states: "6:06 a.m. Long round made. Started at 971 went to 766. Looked and saw Richard Guthrie hanging. Call for back up to cell 973. Deputy [name blacked out] helped me to get him down. We start CPR on him and life squad was called.'

That same log shows that the jailers last made a round known as a short round at 5:22 a.m., and the previous long round had been conducted at 5:00 a.m. These facts indicate that Guthrie wasn't being checked every 20 minutes. More importantly, the incident reports prepared by the deputy jailers contain contradictory information as to whether Guthrie was cut down from the vent, whether the noose was untied, and when the guards last checked on him. Cell 973 was actually an isolation cell and is listed as I-973 on the logs. Another inmate was confined to cell I-972. His identity remains unknown and there is no record that he was ever interviewed about Guthrie's alleged suicide.

The Kenton County Coroner's report states in part that Guthrie was a federal prisoner, and that the type of death suspected is "hanging." The autopsy summarized the circumstances of the death as follows: "Prisoner - in isolation. Last seen @0600 found at 0606 hanging from vent, bed sheet around neck." If the timeline reported to the coroner is correct, and Guthrie was last seen alive at 6:00 a.m. and found dead six minutes later at 6:06 a.m., then he managed to use a bed sheet to hang himself in a span of six minutes. According to forensic experts, it takes six minutes to die from hanging. How then could the jailers not have discovered Guthrie in time to revive him? How could Guthrie have tied the sheet to the vent and then hanged himself for at least six minutes, when he only had a total of six minutes from start to finish?

According to the final report from the Kenton County Coroner dated August 8, 1996: "A post mortem examination was performed on the body of Richard Guthrie at St. Luke's-East on July 12, 1996. The Final Anatomic Diagnosis states: "Body as a whole, Hanging, History of Suspension, Ligature Mark, Comment: The Cause of Death, In My Judgment is Due to Asphyxia Due to Hanging."

Records reveal that Guthrie was not taking any prescription drugs, yet the coroner's laboratory data show that Guthrie had a positive toxicology report. That report disclosed that "high levels of acetaminophen (23 mg/L) were found in blood. Phenypropanolamine and pseudoephedrine were detected in the urine by TLC and GOMS."

The investigations into Guthrie's death were conducted by the Kenton County Sheriff's Department and by the Covington Police Department. According to the Covington Police Department reports, they did very little in the way of an investigation. The initial officer arrived at 6:30 a.m., and his investigation was completed and the case cleared by 8:00 a.m., two hours later. His investigation included viewing the cell and interviewing the two jailers who had discovered Guthrie's body. A crime scene specialist also inspected and photographed cell 973. That person collected as evidence a bed sheet, legal papers, some books, a $20 bill and a sealed envelope. No fingerprints were taken, no fibers were collected, and no testing for blood was done. On the desk in the cell several pills were found. These were never tested, although they were collected and photographed. The specialist arrived at the scene at 6:50 a.m. and left with the detective in charge at 8:25 a.m.

The envelope in Guthrie's cell contained two letters and, according to correspondence from Detective Charles Vallandingham to the U.S. Marshals Service, and his attached report, the letter was: "[A]ddressed to the victim's brother. The letter was opened at HQ by Specialist [name blacked out]. The letter appeared to have been written by the victim and in it he explained to his brother and girlfriend that he was going to commit suicide."

That letter was never tested or examined to determine if Guthrie had actually written it. Guthrie had no documented history of mental illness, depression or suicide attempts. The investigative report by the Covington Police Department states: "This investigation is complete, pending the results of the Autopsy." That report is dated the same day as Guthrie's death. Case opened, solved and closed within the span of a few hours.

Richard Lee Guthrie was a high-profile inmate in the custody of the U.S. Marshals Service. He had been arrested by the FBI and wanted by the Secret Service. He had been involved in a plot to overthrow the U.S. government and was a protected witness waiting to testify against his fellow bank robbers. However, not one single federal law enforcement officer ever verified or investigated the death of Richard Guthrie. That is unheard of in such a situation.

Adding to the intrigue is the fact that Guthrie had been in contact with Judy Pasternak, a reporter with *The Los Angeles Times*, Midwest Bureau. In a letter from the reporter to Guthrie dated three days prior to his death, she invited Guthrie to share his story and unique perspective with her. She played to his ego and commented on their shared suburban Washington, D.C., upbringing. Guthrie had been in contact with Pasternak about his intentions to write a book about the ARA. He even wrote in his unfinished manuscript of a driver he called "Speedie" and "Tim," who had been involved in some of the ARA bank robberies. The tell-all book wasn't completed and never will be. Guthrie's untimely death ended all that he could have revealed about himself, the ARA and the Oklahoma City Bombing.

There is no evidence that Guthrie actually killed himself. He had already made a plea bargain with federal prosecutors in order to shorten his prison sentence for the bank robberies. No serious attempt was made to determine what occurred in cell 973 at the Kenton County Jail. If the Trentadue family had not insisted upon an autopsy when Kenney was alleged to have committed suicide, had they not taken pictures of his tortured body, and had Jesse not undertaken his own investigation, then Kenney Trentadue's death would have been just another so-called suicide by a federal prisoner. Just like Richard Lee Guthrie and Alden Gillis Baker.

Three hangings, all with connections to the Oklahoma City Bombing investigation, each an alleged suicide by an inmate in federal custody. Coincidences? I don't think so, and neither did Jesse Trentadue.

Even for a veteran trial attorney who thought he had seen it all, this was heavy. Jesse Trentadue, relentless seeker of justice for his brother, reluctant sleuth into the Oklahoma City Bombing case, now was looking at a possible serial murder case, targeting federal prisoners

12

Chapter Twelve

A Quest For Answers

It was 2003 when Jesse had that first phone conversation with J.D. Cash. This was post-9/11. The World Trade Center terror strike had eclipsed the Oklahoma City Bombing, with a larger body count and New York City's location at the center of gravity of American prestige in the eyes of the world. There was a new normal in the way America thought about terrorism.

In our small group, there was a new normal too, but this was almost surreal. We now believed – the lawyer, the reporter J.D. Cash and myself, the inmate investigator – that if we could uncover the whole truth, the Oklahoma City Bombing story might turn out to be bigger news than anyone imagined. Behind the federal government's stonewalling about Kenney's death, and the deliberate narrowing of the cast of bombing perpetrators to just McVeigh and Nichols, we believed we glimpsed the shadow of an enormous scandal, one reaching all the way to the upper echelons of official Washington.

Needless to say, we were in a distinct minority. We needed bulletproof evidence to have any of hope of proving a very different reality of the Oklahoma City Bombing from the one everyone knows so well. But we were energized by how far we had come. In our separate circles, we now dug deep for hard evidence that would verify the story Timothy McVeigh told me.

Jesse's principal means of uncovering secrets about the bombing has been the federal Freedom of Information Act. Beginning in late 1995, Jesse has used that law's power over federal agencies to trigger the release of hundreds of documents. Most of these documents have been heavily "redacted," or blacked out, so that confidential names and information are deliberately rendered unreadable. As a result, in some cases, whole documents are indecipherable. But in 2005, in a FOIA lawsuit before U.S. District Court Judge Dale A. Kimball in Salt Lake City, Jesse struck gold.

At first, the FBI denied it had any files responsive to Jesse's very specific request for documents. But Jesse met the FBI stonewall with a courtroom surprise. An FBI insider had leaked him two bombshell teletypes – issued by FBI Director Louis Freeh himself. Under the rules of FOIA, the FBI should have delivered these teletypes when it told the court it had no relevant files.

With egg on their faces, attorneys for the FBI and Justice Department were forced to admit they had been mistaken. Or, in Jesse's opinion: "They flat out lied. They seem to believe that the law and even a court's order doesn't apply to them." Belatedly, the FBI released the documents, in redacted form.

The first teletype was issued by FBI Director Freeh some eight months after the bombing, on January 4, 1996, to a number of FBI field offices. The subject line is: "OKBOMB; EID; MAJOR CASE 117; 0-0: OKLAHOMA CITY." The body of the teletype focuses on the relevance of leads in the bank robbery case for the bombing investigation.

"Prior Bureau communications stated that several common characteristics utilized by the robbers in the BOMBROB investigation included the use of Spanish terminology and the renting of getaway vehicles in the names of prominent FBI officials," Freeh wrote. Also pointed out was the possibility that one of the robbers may have had prior military law enforcement or explosives training.

The teletype also contains several references to an FBI undercover operation at Elohim City before the bombing. For the first time, this teletype contains clear evidence that the informant operation was

Deadly Secrets

conducted by civil rights attorney Morris Dees' organization, the Southern Poverty Law Center.

The four-page teletype discusses a number of SPLC informants, including one from Cincinnati apparently associated with the Midwest Bank Bandits and another at Elohim City. According to the Elohim City informant, before the bombing, McVeigh telephoned Elohim City a number of times, including on April 5, 1995, asking for someone – name redacted – and attempting to recruit others to "assist in the OKBOMB attack." Based on the fact that the redacted person's name contains 23 letters and/or spaces, Jesse concluded the person McVeigh was calling was Andreas Carl Strassmeir. If that assumption is correct, and Strassmeir is the name blacked out, then this teletype appears also to disclose – for the first time – that McVeigh telephoned Strassmeir again on April 17, just two days before the bombing. This second call makes it hard not to at least suspect, as the FBI said it had no reason to, that McVeigh and Strassmeir were somehow associated.

The second teletype from FBI Director Freeh, leaked to Jesse by his secret FBI source, was dated August 23, 1996. This teletype concerns a domestic terrorism investigation being conducted out of the FBI's Philadelphia field office. The subject of the teletype is, again, suspected connections between members of the Aryan Republican Army and Timothy McVeigh.

In this five-page teletype, Director Freeh talks at length about information provided by ARA leader Richard Guthrie after his arrest, including Guthrie having "admitted to paying [someone whose name has been blacked out but is seven letters long – as is M-C-V-E-I-G-H] money derived from bank robberies and identified [again blacked out a person whose name is seven letters long] as an accomplice in certain bank robberies."

This teletype repeatedly refers to "OKBOMB subject Timothy McVeigh" as well as "BOMBROB subjects" – proving that within the FBI a link was clearly being secretly pursued.

This teletype also covers the April 1995 phone calls McVeigh placed to Andreas Strassmeir's residence in Elohim City, as well as an April 16, 1995, telephone call from Strassmeir's residence in Elohim City to

Mark Thomas' home in Pennsylvania, where Stedeford, McCarthy and Guthrie would eventually gather after the bombing.

The teletype also states that there was apparently an informant among this group who "consented to wearing a body recorder and transmitter."

The implications of the FBI and the Southern Poverty Law Center working hand and glove inside Elohim City were stunning, and certainly might suggest why the FBI would want to keep this teletype secret. But J.D. Cash had been hot on the trail of this story for some time. In December 2003, Cash tracked down Morris Dees and questioned him at a press conference at Southeastern Oklahoma University in Durant, Oklahoma. Dees confirmed that someone from his organization was inside Elohim City on April 17, 1995, and that the SPLC "network" had established that McVeigh visited Elohim City multiple times. When Cash pressed Dees to explain what his staff person was doing at a white supremacist training camp, Dees responded: "If I told you what we were doing there, I would have to kill you." Soon after this on-the-fly remark, Dees and the SPLC stopped giving interviews about the Oklahoma City Bombing.

The disclosure of the Louis Freeh teletypes in Jesse's FOIA lawsuit, *Trentadue v. the FBI*, wasn't just a victory. It marked a turning point in Jesse's investigation. He now had conclusive proof that the OKBOMB and BOMBROB cases were clearly connected inside the FBI. Despite its public position to the contrary, the FBI had secretly linked and investigated McVeigh, the ARA and the Elohim City conspiracy. The official story of Timothy McVeigh, lone mastermind of the Oklahoma City Bombing, was beginning to crumble.

Disclosure of the teletypes also left little room for the federal government to credibly argue it had no prior warning of the Oklahoma City Bombing. The FBI Director himself was reporting in these teletypes on an undercover FBI informant operation in place prior to the bombing. Even discounting the other known informant, Carol Howe, who was simultaneously feeding information to the ATF, how is it possible that the FBI did not know what was coming?

By now, though, there was certainly no discounting the advance warning Howe had provided the federal government. Jesse had uncovered a sealed court transcript from a federal prosecution of Howe, and presented it to Judge Kimball in the FOIA case.

On April 24, 1997 – the very same day Timothy McVeigh's trial opened in Denver – Howe's ATF handler Angela Findley-Graham had testified about Howe's informant activities. Findley-Graham was asked specifically about prior warning from Howe. Here is Findley-Graham's testimony:

> Q. And Ms. Howe told you about Mr. Strassmeir's threats to blow up Federal buildings, didn't she?
> A: In general, yes.
> Q: And that was before the Oklahoma City bombing?
> A: Yes.

Findley-Graham was asked about Howe's report of a trip made by Andreas Strassmeir and others from Elohim City to Oklahoma City, presumably to scout the Murrah Federal Building as a potential bomb target. Here is Findley-Graham's testimony:

> Q: And this trip to Oklahoma City by these Elohim City residents occurred before the bombing in Oklahoma City, actually just by about a few weeks, didn't it?
> A: No, it would be months.
> Q: Oh, when did that occur?
> A: The fall of 1994.
> Q: And you are sure about that?
> A: Yes.

But perhaps the most startling testimony from Findley-Graham concerned the fact that the government was not being truthful in the McVeigh prosecution when it said that there were no informants at Elohim City. Here is Findley-Graham's testimony:

> Q: Well, had you heard government statements that there was never an informant at Elohim City in the fall of 1994?
> A: I haven't heard that.

Q: You've never seen those reports that the government took the position in connection with the McVeigh trial –
A: No, I haven't.
Q: You would know that to be untrue though, that statement?
A: Yes, I would know that.

This line of questioning led the government attorney to ask that the proceedings be sealed. The surprising reason: to prevent the information from falling into the hands of the McVeigh defense team. Even more surprisingly, U.S. District Court Judge Michael Burrage granted the motion. "With that McVeigh trial going on, I don't want anything getting out of here that would compromise that trial in any way," the judge said.

The defense attorney immediately asked: "What do you mean by compromise? Do you mean shared with the McVeigh lawyers?" To which the judge gave this shocking reply:

> Yes, or something that would come up, you know. We have got evidence that the ATF took a trip with somebody that said buildings were going to be blown up in Oklahoma City before it was blown up or something of that nature and try to connect it with McVeigh in some way or something.

And so it was that Angela Findley-Graham's testimony, compellingly disputing the government's case against McVeigh as the lone-wolf mastermind, was buried in a Tulsa courtroom, never to be heard by the McVeigh jury. But Jesse's FOIA case exposed this testimony. Together with the Louis Freeh teletypes, the Findley-Graham transcript put solid evidence on the record as to prior government knowledge of the Oklahoma City Bombing from multiple sources.

After reviewing the Louis Freeh teletypes obtained by Jesse, former Deputy Assistant FBI Director Danny Coulson called for reopening the bombing investigation. Coulson was one of the original investigators in the OKBOMB case. J.D. Cash interviewed him in November 2005. During that interview, Coulson stated: "I have had significant experience conducting investigations, and in my view this case is not over." He went on to say: "For years I've believed Elohim City was important to this case, and I think we now know that Tim McVeigh had contacts there. That is key to this complicated case. Any future investigation should focus strictly on McVeigh's associates within that group."

Coulson went further: "Based upon my investigation following the bombing of the Murrah Building on April 19, 1995, and these new documents from the FBI turned up in the Utah case, it's clear to me that further investigation is required. Families of victims and the American people deserve answers to many unanswered questions about the bombing. It is my opinion that a new investigation would only be successful if conducted through the auspices of a federal grand jury."

Coulson continued to speak out regarding the need for a renewed investigation into the bombing. In March 2007, he appeared in a BBC documentary, and while on camera he said: "We have victims here and victims' families, and we don't know the answers. And the answer is frankly a federal grand jury."

While Jesse was pressing his FOIA lawsuit in Salt Lake City, J.D. Cash was working other angles. Cash developed ARA member Peter Langan, now in prison, as a source and, through him, uncovered fresh evidence of just how closely the FBI had tied McVeigh to the ARA. An elaborate web of phone records in the FBI's possession placed McVeigh and various members of the robbery gang in close proximity time and time again, as the bank robbers pulled off their 20-some robberies across the Midwest, beginning the year before the bombing.

Cash learned that the FBI was literally dogging Timothy McVeigh's tracks in search of the ARA connection. A May 1995 memo from the St. Louis office of the FBI instructed its crime lab to compare Timothy McVeigh's shoes, if possible, with shoe impressions taken from the crime scene of an ARA robbery in Maryland Heights, Missouri.

Cash and his writing partner Roger Charles re-investigated another ARA robbery, in Overland Park, Kansas, on September 24, 1994. They discovered that the composite sketch of the robber who accompanied Richard Guthrie that day didn't look anything like his usual partner in crime, Peter Langan. Instead, the sketch bore a remarkable resemblance to Timothy McVeigh. The reporters confirmed

McVeigh was in Wichita 10 days before, because he was caught on videotape selling gold coins there. They also found evidence of phone calls by McVeigh from Marion, Kansas, just two days before the bank job in Overland Park. The reporters sought out Professor Mark Hamm, who has written extensively on the ARA and the bombing case, and he gave his opinion that Guthrie's accomplice that day was McVeigh.

Peter Langan filled Cash in on the FBI's highly unusual processing of the ARA's Ohio safe house after Langan's capture in 1996. Inside, among other promising evidence, the FBI reported finding six blasting caps and two items described as a "Christmas Package." These very possibly belonged to Timothy McVeigh, since he was known to have wrapped blasting caps in Christmas paper for transport across country in his car. Here, well before McVeigh's trial, the FBI had its hands on potentially highly incriminating evidence linking McVeigh and his bomb to the ARA. But instead of closing in, the FBI appeared to look the other way, allowing firefighters to destroy the blasting caps and, presumably, the telltale Christmas packages.

Two more items retrieved from the ARA safe house bear mentioning because of Terry Nichols' disclosures. No one has ever documented a link between Roger Moore and the ARA. Yet inside the safe house in Ohio, again, well before Timothy McVeigh's trial, the FBI found a driver's license that might have done just that. The name on the license was "Robert Miller," which was Roger Moore's gun-show circuit alias. When reporters asked the FBI to see that license, however, the FBI refused to release a copy. According to Langan, there was another link to Moore inside the safe house: a videotape of properties under surveillance by the ARA, including footage of Roger Moore's ranch in Arkansas. Langan says the FBI took that videotape into its possession, but it has never been released.

Danny Defenbaugh, a retired FBI agent who was one of the chief investigators in the OKBOMB case, reviewed FBI documents and reports relating to the ARA bank robberies and their possible connection to the bombing in 2004 at the request of the Associated Press. According to Defenbaugh, neither he nor any of the investigators in the case had ever been informed of the reports or the evidence outlined therein. He went on to say: "If the evidence is still there it should be checked out."

He added: "If I were still in the bureau, the investigation would be reopened."

Others calling for further investigation into the Oklahoma City Bombing case include some of those hardest hit by the bombing: victims and survivors. V.Z. Lawton, who was injured in the blast, is a member of the Oklahoma City Bombing Committee headed by former state Senator Charles Key. That group wants another federal grand jury to investigate all of the evidence that has surfaced. Kathy Wilburn Sanders, who lost her two grandsons, has published a book entitled *After Oklahoma City*, which chronicles her own investigation into the bombing. Jannie Coverdale, who lost her two grandsons in the blast, has become a tireless advocate for further investigation of neglected leads in the case.

One of the mysteries Jannie considers most significant is the so-called "extra leg" recovered from the rubble of the Murrah Building. In the summer of 1995, the Oklahoma State Medical Examiner's Office issued a press release confirming that there was an unidentified left leg, dressed in a combat boot and the remnants of camouflage fatigues, and that the leg probably belonged to a white male. However, several weeks later, after a daylong meeting with federal prosecutors, the FBI and others, the medical examiner's office issued a second press release claiming that it had made a mistake and that the leg in question belonged to a black female.

Eventually, the medical examiner's office determined that the leg belonged to Airman First Class Lakesha Levy, who had been buried in Louisiana. Her body was exhumed. In her casket was a left leg that was detached from her body. The question then became: If that leg wasn't Levy's, whose was it?

When questioned at McVeigh's trial by defense attorney Stephen Jones, Oklahoma State Medical Examiner Dr. Fred Jordan acknowledged that there was an unidentified left leg in the case. He stated: "The truth of the matter is we had eight victims with traumatically amputated left legs missing, and we have nine left legs. We have one too many." Dr. Jordan furthered testified that all attempts to identify the owner of the left leg had failed, and that the identification process even included DNA testing.

McVeigh's defense team had consulted with various experts in forensic pathology in England, who had firsthand experience with bombing cases. The expert who testified at McVeigh's trial was Dr. T.K. Marshall, who is a living legend amongst pathologists. He pointed out to Jones that in his experience, victims' relatives always come forward to claim the remains of their loved ones. Thus unclaimed remains are highly unusual. Dr. Marshall had viewed photographs of the extra leg and studied the medical examiner's reports. At McVeigh's trial, Dr. Marshall gave riveting testimony about the leg, stating: "The working assumption has to be, until excluded, that the leg in question belonged to a bomber."

If the story McVeigh told me was true, that he and Roberto placed Poindexter's body in the back of the bomb truck, it is very possible that the extra leg was just as Dr. Marshall had testified. It belonged to one of the bombers. Jannie Coverdale wants to make sure no one forgets this sensational moment from McVeigh's trial. "That extra leg belonged to one of the bombers, and that was proven in court," she says. "But the government doesn't want anyone to know that because it blows a hole in their official story."

But as Jesse Trentadue knew better than anyone, it would take more than unanswered questions from ex-agents, victims and survivors to overturn a narrative that by 2005 was now an established chapter of American history. To prevail, the citizen investigations would need allies in Washington, D.C. A formidable one was about to enter the story.

From the time of Kenney's death, the Trentadue family began petitioning its local U.S. Congressman, Dana Rohrabacher, from Orange County, California, to look into the case. The Congressman knew of the lengths to which the Trentadue family had gone to find out the truth. Congressman Rohrabacher knew of the family's horrific ordeal and understood the gravity of torture. The Congressman knew that Kenney's mother Wilma paid to have large billboards picturing Kenney's disfigured body posted at bus stops to publicize what had happened. The Congressman knew of Jesse Trentadue's million-dollar wrongful death judgment against the government, and knew that Senator Orrin Hatch of Utah had gone so far as to say, on the record, that Kenney's death looked like murder and smelled like a cover-up.

Duty called, and Congressman Rohrabacher answered in June 2006, by opening a congressional investigation into the Oklahoma City Bombing. "We need to answer some very serious questions in order to have confidence that the truth of this monstrous crime is fully known," the Congressman said. Finally, after all these years, powers that be in Washington, D.C., would re-investigate the bombing and, possibly, shed light on Kenney's death.

Congressman Rohrabacher investigated for six months and filed a sharply worded 14-page report. He concluded that: the FBI ignored credible eyewitness reports on John Doe No. 2, dropped the manhunt for the unidentified McVeigh accomplice too soon, gave Andreas Strassmeir a pass to leave the country when it should have investigated him, and ignored the alarmingly specific warnings of ATF informant Carol Howe about Strassmeir and WAR leader Dennis Mahon casing the Murrah Building on multiple occasions in early 1995. The Congressman made a point of mentioning Kenneth Trentadue by name in the report, noting that the circumstances of Kenney's death were "very disturbing."

To Jesse Trentadue, all of this was familiar ground. But in one vitally important area – the story Timothy McVeigh told me, of his association with the Aryan Republican Army – Congressman Rohrabacher broke new ground, and delivered some sensational evidence.

He and his investigators interviewed Michael Brescia, Scott Stedeford, Peter Langan and Mark Thomas of the ARA, and found serious cause for suspicion. Congressman Rohrabacher reported that in his interview with Langan, he backed away from previous claims to have information about the bombing, and now denied any knowledge. Mark Thomas also denied any knowledge about the bombing, contradicting his previous statements. The committee did not report on its interviews with Brescia or Stedeford, except to say that, over time, the ARA members had changed their stories.

The most stunning information came from the one bank robber the committee could not locate. Kevin McCarthy was missing. Not only that. When the congressional staffers tried to find McCarthy, they confronted an unyielding stonewall at the Justice Department.

Here is how Congressman Rohrabacher reported his staff's painstaking attempts to interview McCarthy:

> Law enforcement officials told subcommittee staff that, after serving 5 years in federal prison for his role in the robberies, McCarthy was released on probation and returned to his native Philadelphia. However, a federal probation officer in Philadelphia could find no record of McCarthy in the federal probation system. A confidential law enforcement source informed the subcommittee that McCarthy was in some type of federal witness protection program and even located him living in Newton, Pennsylvania. When pressed for details a week later, this same source told staff that he could no longer help with this matter, that it was "above his pay grade." Continuing to try and locate McCarthy, the subcommittee chairman contacted the head of the Department of Justice's federal witness protection program. The official confirmed that in the past McCarthy had been in the program but had no information on his current status. Similarly, the subcommittee also discovered, through a private source, that McCarthy is no longer attached to the Social Security Number he had at the time of entry into the federal prison system.

From the extensive details of the search for McCarthy included in the report, it was clear that Congressman Rohrabacher was shocked by the indication that someone inside law enforcement was deliberately hiding this criminal from him. After all, Kevin McCarthy was the man whom Mark Thomas had implicated in the bombing as early as 1997. And later, in a 2007 sworn declaration, Peter Langan would state categorically that he knew McCarthy was one of McVeigh's accomplices on April 19, 1995, that McCarthy lied to the FBI when he presented his purported alibi, and that the FBI knew McCarthy's alibi was false.

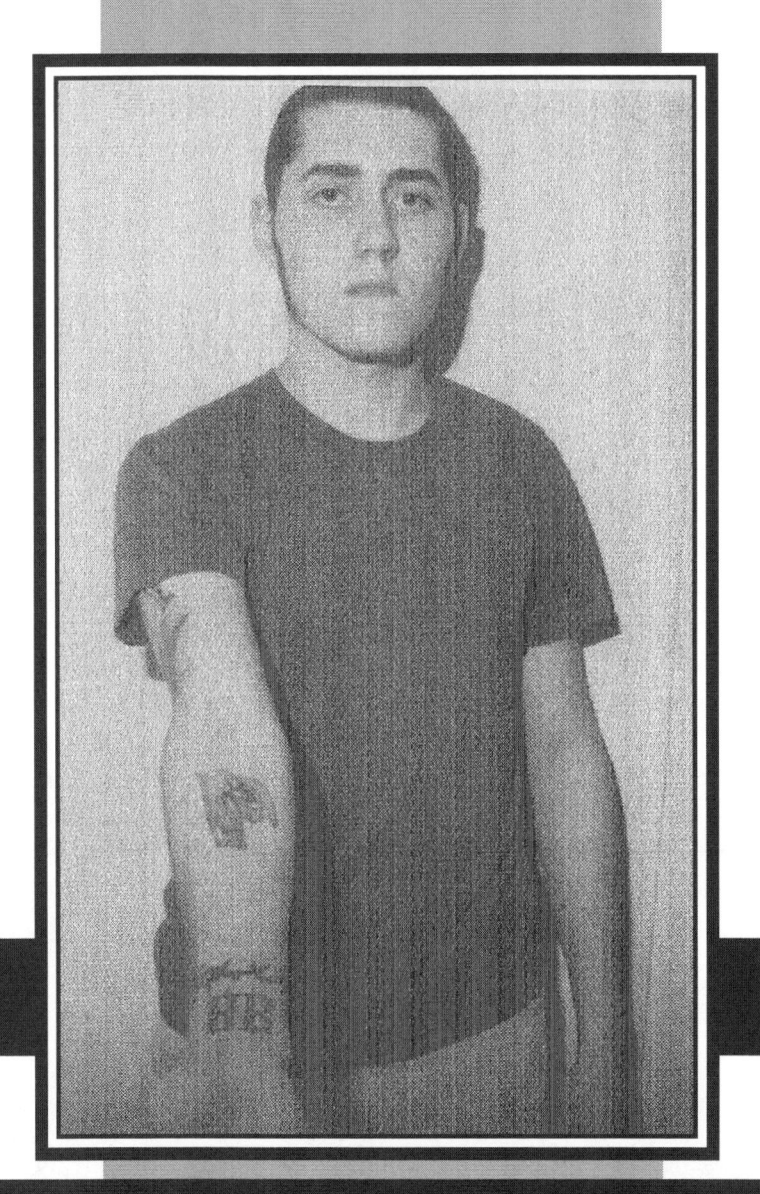

Kevin McCarthy: Missing in 2006

Congressman Rohrabacher didn't hold back in exposing the cover-up. He blasted the Justice Department for hiding McCarthy, and hiding the truth about the Oklahoma City Bombing:

> These facts raise questions about whether McCarthy is, in fact, still under some sort of federal protection as well as why the Department of Justice was unable or unwilling to help find him. It is astonishing that officials from the Department of Justice and other law enforcement agencies were unwilling to permit congressional investigators to question a former bank robber with a possible connection to a large-scale terrorist attack.

For Jesse Trentadue and his investigation, Congressman Rohrabacher's report marked another turning point. The Rohrabacher Report put a congressional stamp on Jesse's long effort. The revised story of the Oklahoma City Bombing had reached Washington, D.C. There, a United States Congressman had boldly begun the rewrite.

Congressman Rohrabacher signed off on his investigation with these memorable words: "This inquiry would have been significantly more complete with greater cooperation from federal law enforcement. Congressional investigators should not face such resistance in doing their job, which is to find the facts and determine the truth."

Finally, the truth seemed to matter to someone in Washington.

It was almost 2007 when the Rohrabacher Report was issued. A milestone date was already on the horizon: April 19, 2010, would mark the 15th anniversary of the bombing. Legal battles, as Jesse well knew from his long career, unfold at a remarkably slow pace. Frequently it takes decades to win such a contest. Sometimes, the battle outlives the warriors. It was time to plan to finish this project.

In one sense, the bombing anniversary was an artificial deadline, but in another, it was imperative. In different ways, this research has engulfed Jesse's life and mine. We have lived and breathed it for many years, Jesse more than I. Reporter J.D. Cash died in 2007. His passing left a hole that can never be filled. All of us close to this investigation carry the dread that we also may go to our graves without the truth.

Afflictions of middle age remind both Jesse and me that the clock is ticking. In 2007, Jesse was diagnosed with Parkinson's disease, a mild case, to be sure, which doesn't slow his demanding trial schedule one bit, but still, is a reminder of mortality. My diabetes continues to take its toll. I've been hospitalized three times with heart trouble, and my eyesight is failing.

Actually, the deadline was my imperative, one result of the year I lived through in 2004, when I came within three days of being executed by lethal injection on June 8, 2004. As Jesse says, he won't quit until he dies. But ever since finishing my book *Secrets Worth Dying For* and receiving an eleventh-hour stay of execution, life looks different to me, even on death row.

I knew I needed closure. So I made a promise to myself, and to Jesse and Kenneth Trentadue. By the time of the 15th anniversary, I would finish my part of our investigation.

Our next move completely backfired. Jesse won approval from Judge Kimball, the judge in the FOIA lawsuit, to take videotaped depositions of Terry Nichols and me so that the judge, and the American public, could decide for themselves whether we were telling the truth about what we know about McVeigh and the bombing.

By now Jesse's theory of the crime against his brother was specific and chilling, and closely followed the outline of McVeigh's story as he told it to me. In *Trentadue v. the FBI*, before Judge Kimball, Jesse charged that the FBI had secretly been part of a sting operation with the Southern Poverty Law Center in Elohim City that targeted McVeigh, Strassmeir and the ARA. After the bombing, FBI agents killed Kenneth Trentadue during a prison interrogation, in the mistaken belief that he was John Doe No. 2.

Relying on this crime theory, Jesse had demanded every piece of paper the FBI had in its files on the various players in the scenario as he laid it out. Over several years, Judge Kimball had reviewed scores of secret documents turned over in the case by the FBI – including some apparently so sensitive that Jesse himself never got to see them. To this day, only the judge and the FBI know what information those documents contain. Based on those documents and other evidence, Judge Kimball approved the depositions. He said he did so because he believed what Nichols and I would say might provide new information Jesse needed to demand more documents – and get them.

To insiders in our investigation, this was a stunning invitation from a federal judge. We knew that whatever secrets the judge had read in those documents about the players in and around Elohim City, they must be dangerous. Judge Kimball went to the outer limits of his jurisdiction to say yes to depositions in a FOIA case. We believe he acted out of grave concern for America.

The depositions never happened. After the FBI and the Justice Department vehemently objected, the U.S. Court of Appeals for the Tenth Circuit overruled Judge Kimball. Once again, Terry Nichols and I were silenced by the very federal agency that stands to be exposed in wrongdoing if we are ever allowed to speak: the Justice Department. Again, that one glaring question: Why? Why would the Justice Department and the FBI go to such extreme lengths just to stop two inmates from telling America their stories?

While Jesse was preparing for the depositions that never happened, he kept the pressure on the government to uncover more documents. In 2008, Jesse filed a fresh FOIA request zeroing in on surveillance videotapes from the day of the bombing, and also on Andreas Strassmeir's possible intelligence connections.

In June 2009, in response to the request relating to Strassmeir, the CIA delivered a sensational response. This seemed to reveal, perhaps beyond any other single piece of evidence Jesse has uncovered, just how monumental are the secrets the government is keeping about the bombing.

The CIA reported that it had found 26 documents that were responsive to Jesse's request focusing on Strassmeir. The CIA was refusing to turn the documents over, however. Here is why: The National Geospatial-Intelligence Agency, which reviewed the documents at CIA request, advised that releasing them "could cause grave damage to our national security."

This was no ordinary FOIA rejection letter. This was code red: The CIA was saying the secrets about Andreas Strassmeir could jeopardize national security.

A few months later, in September 2009, the FBI weighed in with another dramatic response to the other part of Jesse's latest FOIA request: for surveillance tapes made of the Murrah building on the day of the bombing.

Strange but true: As Jesse learned, all these years later, the FBI is still keeping secret hundreds of surveillance tapes. Curiously, except for one clip from one tape, prosecutors did not place these tapes into evidence at the trials of McVeigh and Nichols. What if these tapes captured images of McVeigh accomplices? What if the tapes could positively identify John Doe No. 2, whom witnesses said they saw in the Ryder truck with McVeigh?

None of these questions was answered by the FBI's release of tapes, however. In a development strikingly reminiscent of the most famous government tapes scandal, Watergate, the FBI released only 22 of 244 tapes in its possession, covering only 7 of the 11 camera locations sought by Jesse.

The tapes show the chaos immediately after the bombing. They are blank in the minutes before the blast. These tapes appear to have been edited. Missing were all the tapes Jesse requested from cameras mounted at the front of the Murrah Federal Building, and cameras showing the building's parking lot – in other words, the tapes that would have recorded images of the crime, as opposed to nothing of interest.

Once again, the real story is what is missing: four cameras in four locations going blank at basically the same time on the morning of April 19, 1995. "There ain't no such thing as a coincidence," Jesse said after viewing the tapes. The FBI claims the security cameras did not record just prior to the blast or during the blast because "they had run out of tape" or "the tape was being replaced." One interesting aspect of all the tapes is that they spring back on right after the 9:02 a.m. blast, but there is no footage of the truck pulling up to the building, parking, or of the passenger exiting the truck, as seen by eyewitnesses. According to Jesse: "The absence of footage from these crucial time intervals is evidence that there is something there that the FBI doesn't want anybody to see."

As Jesse's campaign for release of the tapes continued in the months leading up to the 15th anniversary of the bombing, Jesse pressed harder, demanding to inspect unedited videotoapes, and confronting Justice Department lawyers with photographic evidence of cameras mounted

Deadly Secrets

on the Murrah Building the morning of the bombing, cameras that would have captured the Ryder truck.

Jesse had some more leverage to turn up the pressure: a Secret Service log that describes a missing video sequence from one of the tapes that has apparently been edited. An entry in this log, written by a Secret Service agent on April 24, 1995, references "suspects" – plural – exiting the Ryder truck 3 minutes and 6 seconds before the bomb blast.

Suspects, plural? Whoa. Timothy McVeigh and ... who else? McVeigh supposedly delivered the bomb in the Ryder truck by himself, with no passenger. And Terry Nichols was in Kansas that day.

For Jesse, the answer was as simple as it was explosive. The man caught on tape getting out of the truck with McVeigh was Richard Guthrie: John Doe No. 2 and, most unluckily for Kenneth Trentadue, a man who shared so many physical traits with Kenney, it may have cost him his life.

That tape was a prize worth fighting over, and Jesse clearly had another fierce fight on his hands. But he was already pondering a most interesting possibility – a way to move his investigation to another level.

If Jesse could prove to U.S. District Judge Clark Waddoups in the FOIA case that the FBI edited or altered one of the surveillance tapes, or held onto one or more tapes it should have turned over, that would prove bad faith. Such a ruling could open the door to FBI subpoenas – and to America finally learning the whole truth about who was with McVeigh in the Ryder truck.

There is no statute of limitations on murder.

13

Chapter Thirteen

Writing On The Wall

It's April. A famous poet called this the cruelest month.

The 15th anniversary of the Oklahoma City Bombing is now just days away. A grief-stricken circle of mourners with permanent gaping holes in their lives will soon gather at the haunted space that once was the Alfred P. Murrah Building to remember their dead.

Jannie Coverdale will be there for Aaron and Elijah, who would be 20 and 18 now if they hadn't been slaughtered at ages 5 and 3 by the bomb blast that destroyed America's Daycare Center, on the second floor of the Murrah Building.

Jannie had every reason to believe this was the safest place in the world for her two little grandsons. But the daycare center wasn't safe from Timothy McVeigh. The bomb killed 19 children under the age of 6. Jannie Coverdale, like many other survivors, will never forget the horror of discovering what had happened. "I took off running, and two of my co-workers went with me," she says. "We ran up on the 4th Street side. The damage to the building wasn't too bad. But then we went around on 5th Street. The building, including the daycare center, was gone."

For many of the survivors, downtown Oklahoma City holds horrible and everlasting memories. Kathy Wilburn-Sanders, grandmother of Chase and Colton, ages 2 and 3, says that the debris from the blast "entombed the children" and that the Murrah Building became the "deathbed of its victims." All the survivors I have spoken to define their lives by the date and time of the blast. There are only two periods of time for them, before April 19, 1995, and after. Kathy's accounts of the moments and days after the bombing, before the bodies of her grandsons were located and identified, are filled with references to time, losing time and experiencing time as agony. She says her last memories of Chase and Colton are "etched" in her mind "forever."

Jannie Coverdale will never forget the moment she learned her grandsons were dead. She had been sitting in a church for most of four long days, waiting for news with other families whose husbands, wives and children were missing. "I remember screaming at God," she says. "I remember telling Him that I would never serve Him again, because I had begged Him to just let them be alive. ... I remember going into another room in the church and looking out of the window, and, as far as I could see, I saw nothing but sadness, and I knew I was seeing into the future, and that was my life I was looking at."

The Oklahoma City Bombing National Memorial, where the survivors will commemorate their loved ones on the anniversary of the bombing, contains 168 chairs, each with the name of a victim. The chairs mark each victim's approximate location at the time they died. Light shines from underneath each empty chair at night. The Gates of Time mark the space in front of the Murrah Building where the Ryder truck bomb detonated. Two 13-ton yellow bronze structures resembling doors are marked with inscriptions over the entrances to the memorial grounds. The inscription on the east reads, "9:01 AM," and the one on the West, "9:03 AM." The moment of the explosion, 9:02 AM, isn't memorialized.

A lovely elm tree spreads its branches protectively over one area of the courtyard. This has become known as the "Survivor Tree" because it miraculously withstood the devastating blast, when whole buildings around it were destroyed. The tree symbolizes the courage of those who lived on after the bomb.

Even here, however, at ground zero of the official story of the bombing, there is a reminder that something is wrong with this picture. On a wall of the old *Journal Record Newspaper* building that survived the blast, a team of first responders memorialized their shocked reaction, graffiti-style: "Team 5, 4-19-95. We Search For the truth. We seek Justice. The Courts Require it. The Victims Cry for it. And GOD Demands it!"

The bombing memorial and grounds are stately, impressive and grand in the way of heroic federal monuments. But these raw words – scrawled by rescuers who were witnessing human horror they could never have imagined – go to the heart of the matter. For some survivors, this is the real memorial, because 15 years after the fact, it stands as a stern reminder that the whole truth has not been found, and justice has not been done.

Over the years, Ruth Schwab, a victim, has reluctantly come to share this belief. Ruth was a coworker of V.Z Lawton, at the federal Housing and Urban Development Department office in the Murrah Building. She was badly disfigured in the bombing. She lost an eye and underwent reconstructive surgery. Weirdly, years afterward, she remembers glass pushing its way out of her body one day in the shower. "It hurts right before it comes out," she says. "I will always feel the effects … They will not go away."

All of this makes it especially hard for Ruth to face the belief she has come to: that, somehow, the government that was supposed to protect her, knew about the Oklahoma City Bombing in advance, and allowed it to happen.

Ruth says she tried for years to ignore what she was hearing about a cover-up, but eventually the information became too much to ignore. "The fact is that they knew there was going to be a bomb," she says. "Everyone knew! … That blows me away. The day-care. They could have done something … anything … That was a heart-breaker."

As always, my experience of the anniversary of the bombing will be very different from that of the mourners, because of where I sit. They, I imagine, will mostly be remembering the nightmare: where they were at 9:02, how they found out, burying their dead. But I wasn't there. The part I witnessed was the retribution, in June of 2001, when Timothy

McVeigh walked past my cell here on death row and gave me the nod on his way to the death chamber.

Sometimes, when I think about that moment, I still wonder if Timothy McVeigh was really executed at all. One of the reasons he made the bargain with me that he did, to tell his story, was that he needed an experienced jailhouse lawyer to help prevent the autopsy on his body that was standard procedure after an execution. That was my end of the bargain, and I kept it. There was no autopsy on Timothy McVeigh.

I don't know whether it was his paranoia, or something more, but as McVeigh's execution date approached, he told me he wasn't sure he was going to die. He spoke of a scenario in which the Major or members of his team would infiltrate the execution process and replace the lethal drugs with other substances. According to McVeigh, the CIA and other U.S. agencies involved in covert missions have developed drugs that create the illusion of death in the human body and disguise all signs of life. These drugs would be administered in the execution process. Once McVeigh's body was released to his legal representative, a squad of medical personnel would revive him. He would then undergo reconstructive surgery, and be rewarded for his efforts and loyalty to those he served.

Sometimes, when think I about "Operation Elm Tree," which was the code name prison administrators gave McVeigh's execution, this outlandish scenario pops to mind. A memorandum from one of McVeigh's lawyers, dated August 30, 1995, raises a similar possibility. That memo, prepared by Randy Coyne, reports that McVeigh raised the "possibility of a plea bargain. He said the government could use me for a special mission. They could say they executed me. They want to punish me. They wouldn't have to worry about losing me. . ." According to Coyne, McVeigh acknowledged that this scheme had an extremely remote chance, but said, "I won't deny it's a possibility."

This is far-fetched for sure, but it does reveal McVeigh's mindset very early on, just days after his indictment, before the elaborate grooming and massaging of his role in the bombing in preparation for his trial.

Jannie Coverdale was one of survivors who watched the execution on closed circuit TV in Oklahoma City – at the Federal Transfer Center, as a matter of fact, where Kenney Trentadue was killed. Jannie describes the execution this way: "I sat in that room and watched Tim, and I still don't know if he's dead or not. He was covered from his feet to his neck with a white sheet. We couldn't see his arms, so we don't know if anything was going on or not. What I do know is that his eyes were open, after he was supposed to have died. I've heard all kinds of tales. But I believe that had he been working for the government, then he is still alive."

Another witness, Chrissy Titsworth Luna, remembers it differently: "I watched the man die via closed circuit at the Federal Transfer Prison in Oklahoma City. And that sorry SOB, when asked if he had anything to say, just turned his head to the right, then left and looked up and said nothing, and they injected him, and you could see him trying to fight off the sleeping agent and blowing out his mouth and then it was over . . . that fast. Before he died he told his Dad, 'I could tell them I'm sorry, but I'd be lying.'"

Two eyewitnesses, two different takes. If we knew for sure which was right, we'd be that much closer to the truth. If, if, if. This fascinating, spiraling investigation might best be summed up as The Big If. I admit there were times along the way when I thought Jesse and I were close to solving the Oklahoma City Bombing. Instead, what we have accomplished, I believe, is something else – something remarkable.

After 15 years of investigating, we have opened up the deepest, darkest cold case of all time, the most mysterious unsolved mystery, the mother of all true crime stories.

The clues to crack this case are here, inside this book. A treasure trove of them are waiting to give up secrets to forensic examination, from boxes of explosives that might be tied to the bombing, to hundreds of surveillance tapes of the Murrah Building that might contain images of John Doe. No. 2, to ARA surveillance videotape of Roger Moore's ranch, to the handprint, mystery blood spot and writing on the wall of Kenneth Trentadue's cell, to rental records on multiple Ryder trucks and, most astoundingly, to the "extra leg" from the Murrah Building rubble that Timothy McVeigh's story suggests belonged to the man who built the bomb.

The list of leads is long, extremely inviting and virtually untouched by professional investigative hands. Bottom line: Contrary to what the FBI has kept very quiet until now, the Oklahoma City Bombing case is not closed. What is needed now, to solve it and finally answer the cry for justice on the wall, is a serious investigation by a body powerful enough to force the FBI to give up its deadly secrets.

These secrets have been well kept by a long parade of confidential government informants, who were paid both for their information and their silence. But there are so many of them, who know so much about the matters we have investigated. It only takes one person speaking out to break the chain of silence. Someone knows who was behind the Oklahoma City Bombing. Someone knows who killed Kenneth Trentadue. In the right hands, the evidence in this book will lead straight to that person.

My hope, for the sake of Kenney, who very possibly was Victim No. 169, is that someone with subpoena power will reflect on the facts as they are presented here, and take action.

With some measure of closure, I can now say that my work on this case is complete. I have reported the story Timothy McVeigh told me, and verified the information I could. I am well aware that my prisoner status challenges my credibility from word one. That is why I have relied heavily on documents to test the McVeigh story, so readers can judge it for themselves.

As for Kenneth Trentadue's death – and possibly Guthrie's and Baker's as well – I have followed the fascinating leads McVeigh provided as far as I could. As a prisoner myself, Kenney's case cried out to me from the moment I first read about it. What happened to Kenney is every prisoner's worst nightmare.

When I volunteered to help Jesse get to the bottom of Kenney's case, I did so out of a prejudice I won't deny. No man, no matter what he's done, should face a squad of federal police at 3:00 in the morning, alone in a cell with no way to defend himself, leaving behind nothing but a bloody handprint on the wall, where he died grasping desperately for a panic button just out of reach.

What Kenney Trentadue had done wrong, it should be remembered, was to have a few beers after work when his parole officer said don't. This isn't supposed to happen in America. This is why prisoners everywhere know Kenney's name and what happened to him. In prison-speak, it's called "getting Trentadued."

Finding a way to tell this story has been challenging. Reporters can't interview me. A federal court of appeals blocked my offer to tell my story via videotaped deposition, so the public could see and hear me and judge for themselves.

Last fall, I confronted one more roadblock. In September 2009, two men who identified themselves as FBI agents visited me here on Federal Death Row.

They had something to offer me – my life.

It went like this. If I would not publish this book, the Justice Department would halt its effort to seek the reinstatement of the death penalty in my case. Otherwise, and I quote: "We will use the full might of the federal government against you."

This book is my answer.

I have already received more than I have given from my work on this case with Jesse Trentadue. He is a loyal brother to Kenney and a true friend to me. Through our work together, and especially my writing of this book, I have experienced something almost miraculous.

Even on death row, the truth will set you free.

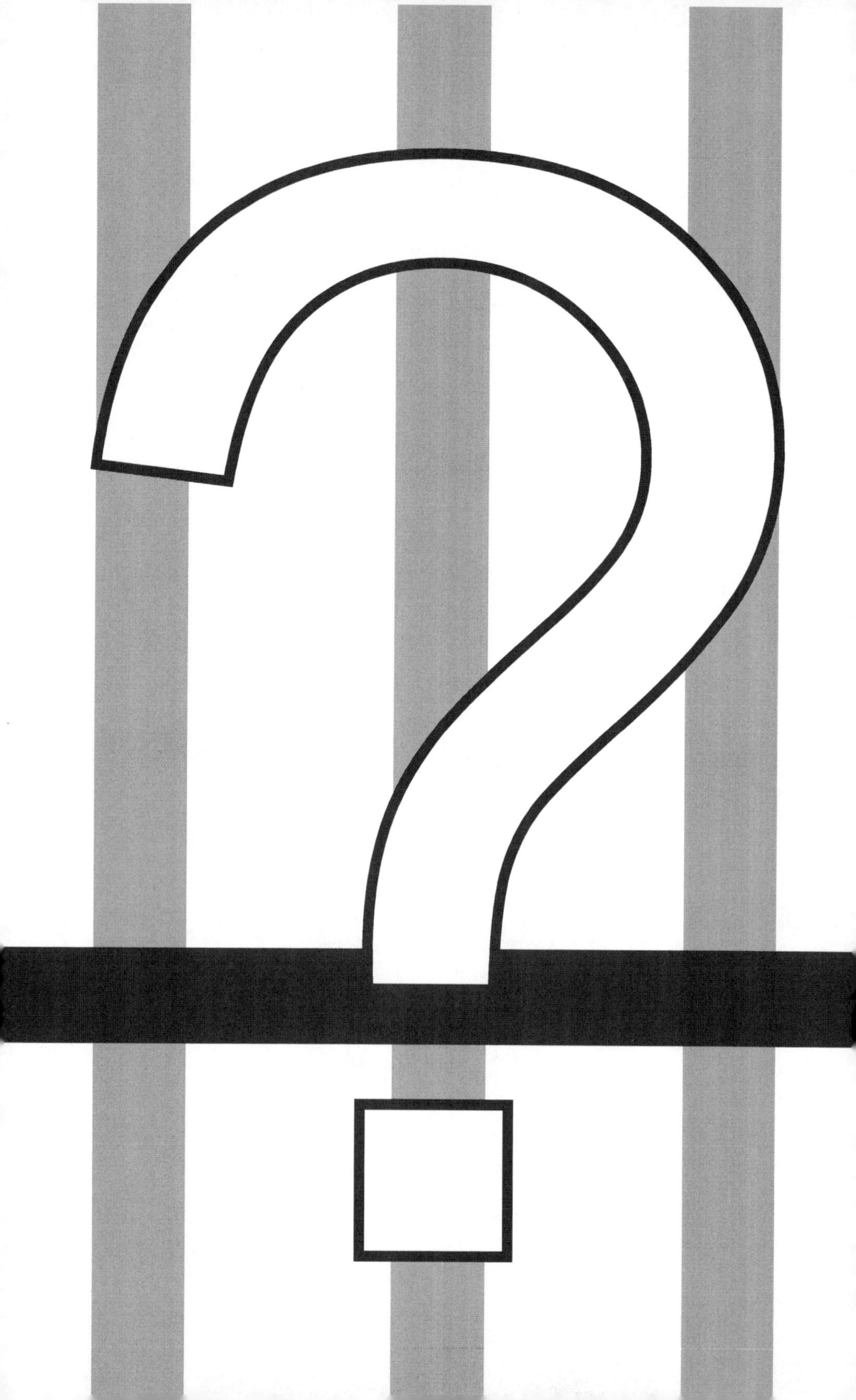

SOMEONE KNOWS

Someone who will read this book knows the answers to the mysteries investigated in these pages:

Who were Timothy McVeigh's accomplices, who were never brought to justice in the Oklahoma City Bombing?

Who killed Kenneth Trentadue in the federal detention center in Oklahoma City on August 21, 1995?

Victims and survivors of the Oklahoma City Bombing deserve to know the truth. They need your help.

www.deadly-secrets.com

Sources will remain anonymous.

About the Author

Death row inmate David Paul Hammer is a criminal legend. After a childhood in Oklahoma marked by poverty and abuse, Hammer left home at age 14. He worked odd jobs, became addicted to drugs, got married, fathered a child, and wound up in prison at 19 for robbery and a violent hostage-taking incident. Except for two escapes, he has been incarcerated ever since.

In prison, Hammer developed into a master con artist, using a brilliant mind to conduct lucrative, imaginative scams from his prison cell. But he also furthered his education by earning his GED and collegiate associate degrees in criminal justice, psychology and paralegal studies. He is a skilled jailhouse lawyer and social activist.

By 1984, Hammer had accumulated a staggering 1,230-year sentence for various crimes. In 1996, he killed a cellmate and received the death penalty. That set the stage for a strange twist of fate. David Paul Hammer of Oklahoma and Timothy McVeigh, the Oklahoma City Bomber, would soon become fellow inmates on Federal Death Row in Indiana.

During the two years leading up to McVeigh's execution in 2001, Hammer observed McVeigh closely, talked to him in depth about his crime, and took notes. Hammer was ready to put his considerable talents to use in the writing of this book.

Hammer has written two previous books: *The Final Escape*, his autobiography, and *Secrets Worth Dying For: Timothy McVeigh and the Oklahoma City Bombing*. In 2004, Hammer came within three days of death by lethal injection, before an appeals court granted him a stay of execution. His case is still pending.

Acknowledgments

I am indebted to so many people for this book. I could never have written it without the assistance from people on the outside. I want to especially thank Jesse C. Trentadue, who has become my brother and my friend. Without his guidance and investigative efforts we wouldn't have uncovered as much as we have so far. Many journalists have assisted me over the years, but none more so than J.D. Cash and Lt. Colonel Roger Charles (U.S. Marines Retired). They have reported on the Oklahoma City Bombing since day one. They shared their knowledge, writings and opinions with me and they verified many facts for me. We lost J.D., but his spirit and memory lives on and he will never rest in peace until the truth behind Oklahoma City is exposed.

In recent years the investigative efforts of Wendy S. Painting have allowed me to be secure in my command of the facts that McVeigh told me. She has spent considerable time, resources and more interviewing witnesses and reviewing the McVeigh defense file at the University of Texas in Austin. She has generously provided me with copies of documents that I could never have obtained on my own.

A very special debt of gratitude goes to Jannie Coverdale. Jannie is an extraordinary woman. Her strength, wisdom and kindness show through to all who meet her. She means the world to me. I value her friendship and I am forever grateful to her.

I also want to thank André Kellner and Eva, for all of their efforts to make this book a reality. They continue to work on my behalf to insure that the world knows about this book. And, last but certainly not least, I want to thank Debbie Ashton. Her skills and knowledge have made the writing process much easier. I'm most grateful.

To the many others who have helped me with this project, I thank you.